The optimal *negotiator*

A Companion for Serious Deal Makers

Dr. James G. Murray

©2002 **optimal solutions** *international*
Maxwell, Ontario, Canada

Helping people and organizations
achieve their full potential.

Discounts are available on bulk orders. Contact the publisher directly:
(519) 924-2084; Fax (519) 924-2044.
Or order via Internet at www.optimal-negotiator.ca

Cover art and design by John Silva.
Page layout and assembly by John Silva.
Printed in Canada by Allprint Ainsworth Associates Inc.

First printing, November 2002

Canadian Cataloguing in Publication Data

Murray, James G. (James Gibson)
The optimal negotiator: a companion for serious deal makers

ISBN 0-9680627-1-7
1. Negotiation. I. Title.
BF637.N4M87 2002   302.3   C00-900651-6

For Anne.

NOTES

On Brevity: Despite the obvious scope of the topic, a concerted effort has been made to ensure both brevity and simplicity. For ease of reading, there are no footnotes and, despite a vast literature, a bibliography has not been included. For the more devoted reader, a listing of resource materials may be found on the companion web site for the Internet course of the same name (*www.optimal-negotiator.com*).

On Gender: I acknowledge that both women and men negotiate. That is why reference is made to both genders. However, constant reference to both he and she (and derivatives of same) in the same sentence, can make for awkward reading. Accordingly, I have referred to the two genders in balance throughout the text. The reader can feel free to substitute one for the other.

On Inferring Reality: The reader should neither assume nor infer that real people or events have been used to illustrate key points, although the negotiating situations depicted might appear familiar. For the most part, the examples and advice given reflect the personal opinions of the author by virtue of his research and unique experiences. Any characterizations, names ascribed or descriptions made of either people or events that might appear to resemble real situations or individuals are wholly unintentional.

On Acknowledgements. This book draws from a lifetime of eclectic experience and learning. I am indebted to special friends whose unstinting generosity, candour and humour enriched my life and thus my writing. I pay heed as well to those rare foes along the way who likewise strengthened my character.

CONTENTS

45. Persistence can pay huge rewards.

46. Read their signals.

47. Objections are masked opportunities.

48. Be wary of assumptions.

49. How you say it is important.

50. The best concessions may cost nothing.

51. Make the pressure explicit.

52. Agendas are assets worth having.

53. The first offer is not the final offer.

54. A change can break an impasse.

55. Deadlock is not a dirty word.

56. Know when to close.

57. Close with magic.

58. Critically assess your performance.

59. Practice when it doesn't count.

60. Avoid dialogues of the deaf.

61. Craft a message that appeals.

62. Be a non-directional listener.

63. Ask the right questions.

64. Learn the language of hidden meanings.

65. All of you is communicating.

66. A tactic perceived is no tactic.

67. Leverage the power of your team.

68. Choose your team carefully.

69. Team size matters.

70. Price is a point of view.

71. Price and terms are symbiotic.

72. Reinforce your opening.

73. Deadlines are of your own making.

74. When you don't know what to do, do nothing.

75. Always write the agreement.

76. Exceptions disprove the rule.

77. Promote your credibility.

78. Negotiate with decision makers.

79. Humanize yourself.

80. Trade expendables to achieve essentials.

81. If it seems "too good," it probably is.

82. Acknowledge gender differences.

83. Listen for telltale traps.

84. Say "yes" when you're happy.

85. Risk-taking is its own reward.

86. Heed the 90:10 rules.

87. You have to enjoy it to be good.

88. These things you NEVER do.

FOREWORD

This is a book about enhancing the quality of your life. Applying its practical wisdom to your personal and business negotiations will make a measurable difference in your future endeavours as well as in important relationships.

The **optimal**_negotiator_ is based on over 30 years of accumulated research, teaching and applied experience in virtually every negotiating arena – from complex corporate transactions and collective bargaining to everyday encounters with people just like you. The author has designed and taught courses on basic and advanced negotiating skills on university campuses, in plant cafeterias and corporate board rooms across North America. Over 400,000 people from all walks of life have participated in his highly acclaimed program, _The Art of Negotiating...with anyone_.

An adult educator by training, Jim Murray believes that success flows from an understanding of some fundamental and profound truisms. For him, the object of life is to simplify rather than "complexify" the basic principles that enable us to achieve our aspirations and make a real difference in everything we do. Many intellectually brilliant people fail to appreciate the value of common sense. The fundamental purpose of The **optimal**_negotiator_ is therefore to give you the simple, common sense principles that are the foundation of the winning edge.

Jim Murray is convinced that mastery requires self-confidence. Reaching that ultimate level of skill and knowledge is achieved through conscious reflection on the key principles and insights espoused by optimal negotiators and then, through dedicated practice and continued refinement, adapting them to our unique strengths and capabilities.

Some people rarely travel without a road map. The **optimal** *negotiator* can be your road map to better deals. Keep this handy reference tool nearby and seek its guidance whenever the need arises ... as inevitably it will. And customize its counsel by adding your own notes, experiences and observations to the pages that follow.

In keeping with his commitment to simplify, the author's time-tested discoveries and insights are presented in an easy-to-read, abbreviated fashion. Digest his invaluable advice, thoughtfully, in bite-sized chunks whenever your negotiating challenges dictate. In time, with patient application, you will discover the significance and relevance of these lessons for winning.

If you cannot negotiate, you cannot solve your problems. If you can't solve your problems, you can't control your life nor can you grow, either personally or professionally. Therefore, it follows, you cannot become your best, or what you may be destined to become. And, if that doesn't happen, you will never be completely happy with your life.

Learning how to negotiate the optimal way is a journey toward personal fulfillment and happiness. For what else really matters?

1   Always distinguish wants from needs.

Negotiations begin with an articulation of wants. The initial position espoused is invariably a statement of what the negotiators would like to achieve, not what they can "live with." Artful negotiating is a process of identifying and satisfying the needs of the other party, not capitulating to the initial outline of wants.

To illustrate, consider our wants and needs when it comes to something as basic as transportation. The primary requirement is surely to arrive at the intended destination safely. While I would prefer to travel in style and comfort, if not luxury, the basic need is to simply "get there," hopefully in a timely fashion. So, while I might desire to drive (or perhaps be chauffeured) in an expensive automobile, my principle concern is for reliable transportation, which can be adequately met with a less extravagant vehicle. Indeed, a bicycle will do. Or, if there is no alternative, I could walk.

Similarly, when an opposing negotiator begins by asking for something you feel is outrageous or beyond your means, calm yourself and consider this critically important question: "What is she really asking for?" Consider both the personal and organizational needs that might lie behind the opening proposition. Understand that the first number in a negotiation is never the final number. Take the time to discover her interests, motivations and aspirations. This is what she says she wants; what is it that she really needs?

The challenge of discovering and defining a negotiator's deeper, driving needs is that very few people really know what their

Always distinguish wants from needs.

basic needs are. They're much more focussed on what they'd like to see happen. And even when they do know what their needs are, they are unlikely to tell you at the outset of your negotiation. To discover the needs of your alter negotiator, you must know how to artfully question, probe and encourage a definition of wants.

Like most things you'll discover about the art of negotiating, the best approach to ascertaining needs is not that difficult. Just ask a few simple, straightforward questions, like: "Why do you want that?" Or, "What are you going to do with it?" By discovering the reasons that lie behind the wants, and by learning more about her personal interests, aspirations and objectives, you will have begun to ascertain and understand the needs that drive the expression of wants.

Although we may articulate the same or similar wants, we are not motivated by the same fundamental needs. That's why win-win deals are always possible.

Seek first to understand before you can be understood.
— Stephen Covey

2

2 "No" is just a position in time.

In a negotiation, "no" is never final until or unless you accept it as final.

"No" means different things to different people and it means different things at different times. To a child, "no" is an open invitation to challenge parental authority. To an unquestioning subordinate, it's rejection carved in stone. To a literalist, it's a lost opportunity. To a pessimist, it's a way of life. To the optimal negotiator, it's just a position in time. (And, in a negotiation, time changes everything.)

Depending on its timing, the exact phrasing, context and non-verbal support, "no" can have a multitude of possible meanings: I'm not sure; I don't understand; I need more information; it's the wrong time; or, perhaps, I need more time. None of these meanings implies a categorical denial of your position or a rejection of your needs.

"No" is often a tactic (and should therefore be perceived as such), used consciously as well as unconsciously, to either lower expectations or to misdirect. It might signify an objection to a part of your argument rather than the whole. Keep in mind that objections and reservations are neither interruptions nor rejections but an integral part of the negotiating process. Curiously, objections can signal a genuine interest in the proposals under discussion and thus should be viewed (and treated) as an effort to understand or clarify.

Optimal negotiators know that "no" can be used strategically to elevate an opponent's happiness level. It is an axiom of

"No" is just a position in time.

human behaviour that the harder you work to earn something, such as a concession, the greater is your sense of accomplishment or victory whenever that objective is achieved.

How do you feel when you ask for something you believe you might not get, at a price that seems unreasonably high, and the immediate response is agreement with your request? Are you happy? Not likely. Conversely, if the initial reaction is "no" but, after an investment of time and effort, you achieve most of what you seek, are you not happier? Of course you are.

To find openings for advancing the discussion and thus also your interests, endeavour to discover the reasons behind the "no." Don't legitimize "no" by accepting it at face value. Pace the process by asking questions or momentarily changing the topic. If she objects to your price, focus the conversation on the terms and conditions. Keep in mind that she too may also be seeking to find a way around the "no."

Be creative and be persistent. Remember, "no" is an integral part of the negotiating process. Indeed, without it, there is no negotiation.

We are surrounded on all sides by insurmountable opportunities.
– Pogo

3 People need time to accept new ideas.

When should you ask for that which you really want, especially if your position is a difficult one for the other party to accept? The answer is: right at the outset of the negotiation. And, when you do, expect the obvious response: "No. You can't have it."

Negotiators obviously start the process with opposing points of view. The objective, of course, is to change that point of view. When positions are far apart or seem intractable, this can take some time. But two basic principles are working in your favour. The first is that negotiating is an investment of time and effort. And the return on that investment is that time changes everything. The second principle is that "giving gets." In the *quid pro quo* discussion that ensues, your alter negotiator will soon discover the necessity to modify his position as a means of encouraging you to accept it.

Even the most brilliant ideas are rejected at the outset – largely because they have not been contemplated before. The philosopher, John Stuart Mill, once observed that "Every great movement must experience three stages: ridicule, discussion and adoption."

Don't become dispirited when you hear your opening position rejected. Remind yourself that he likely has never thought about your novel concept before, that he needs time to "sleep on it" or, perhaps, to discuss it with others. Consider also that you have yet to hear his reasons for opposing your idea. Perhaps it's a notion he doesn't fully understand or maybe he has some concerns that you need to address.

People need time to accept new ideas.

People become comfortable with new or difficult ideas by going through a necessary mental transition. While they don't immediately embrace "yes" for many reasons, they typically begin the transition through the expression of a qualified "maybe" – as in "Let me think about that" or "I'll talk with Harry" or "We'll study it and get back to you." None of these responses implies disagreement, just that acceptance of the proposition requires more time. The responses do signify progress. And that is your primary objective in a negotiation – to gradually and gracefully advance the discussion towards the desired outcome.

Conversely, when you hear a new idea or a difficult request, how should you respond? Start with the qualified "maybe." This conveys the impression that you are flexible and open-minded (even though you disagree with their position). This response, rather than an outright rejection, will make your opponent more receptive to your ideas. It will also protect your reputation should you eventually have to disagree with an unacceptable request or demand.

He that wrestles with us strengthens our nerves and
sharpens our skills. Our antagonist is our helper.
– Edmund Burke

4

The less you care,
the better the deal.

The greater your desire to acquire or achieve something, the higher will be the price you must pay to do so.

You will always pay more for those things you feel you must have, be it the powerful red sports car you always dreamt of owning or that one-of-a-kind house with the picture-book white picket fence around it. In a negotiation, we all too easily become the unthinking victims of our wants, emotions and aspirations.

Optimal negotiators have learned through experience the value of being, or appearing to be, dispassionate. They have developed an ability, if not a comfort zone, in feigning indifference. They understand the wisdom and value of objectivity in negotiations. They know that there are always different ways to satisfy their objectives and that determination may involve another time and place. They appreciate that when your alter negotiator discovers you absolutely "must have it," she will exact a higher price.

The tendency to become emotionally involved with the deal is largely a function of inexperience. As we get older, we come to the realization that, more often than not, there is "another one" – a comparable choice – and often a better one, to be had. We learn through experience, sometimes painful, that the prize we covet (whether the valued object be a car, a house, a job or something else we care a great deal about) is not the only one of its kind. And when we find those different and alternative ways of satisfying our needs, we discover that we really do have options. In negotiating, having options is having power.

The less you care, the better the deal.

Another way of looking at this principle is to appreciate that the more you care (about what you seek), the less power you have to achieve it. In a relationship, for example, the person who is most committed to the quality of the union has the least amount of leverage when differences arise. Sad, perhaps, but also true.

In a negotiation, everything has a 'price' or a value ascribed. And that price is entirely dependent upon the point of view and the needs of the buyer and the seller. The right price is the amount a willing buyer will pay and a needy seller will accept.

Don't make your true feelings about the object you covet a part of the price equation. Strive to be objective in your assessment of realistic options and alternatives. If you cannot be dispassionate about the preferred outcome, you will have little or no choice but to pay the (higher) price and thus the added cost of your own emotional involvement.

Success lies not in how quick you work but rather in where you choose to focus your attention.

5

Aspirations are
self-fulfilling.

If you truly believe something will happen, the likelihood of it happening is considerably enhanced. Norman Vincent Peale called this principle the power of positive thinking.

"Can do" thinking applies to virtually any human undertaking. But its application at the bargaining table is profound. Indeed, the depth of your belief in your price or your position, and thus your commitment to achieving it, can prove more powerful in the final analysis than your negotiating experience or skill.

When you are utterly convinced of the appropriateness of your price (as opposed to feigning support for what you, in fact, know to be an unrealistic number), you ultimately prevail in convincing the other party of its validity. Likewise, when you genuinely believe in the uniqueness of your product or the value of your service, you will become a much better and more persuasive salesperson. If you truly think your organization is the very best there is, you will be its greatest ambassador.

Poor negotiators are those who listen to and are persuaded by their own negative self-talk. Certainly, there are times when we have doubts, when that "voice within" tells us why we can't do something. To overcome this debilitating human tendency you need to nurture a high aspiration level. This you do by focusing your attention on why you can achieve your objectives, not why you can't.

Aspirations are self-fulfilling.

A high aspiration level evolves and is reinforced through testing, challenging and exploring the other's position rather than accepting it at face value. It flows from giving yourself greater latitude in your opening position than you might traditionally provide. It is a consequence of having done your homework thoroughly – by having prepared artful, probing, intelligent questions and by having developed good answers for the tough questions that invariably will be asked. In life and therefore in negotiations, preparation is the means by which you "psyche up" and reinforce your aspiration level.

Research suggests that positive expectations beget positive outcomes. Great performers, regardless of their arena of endeavour or competition, never doubt their ability to perform to their highest expectations. Given their unstinting conviction in the power and potential of their talents, they seek only to do better each time out. As someone has observed, it is their attitude that determines their altitude – how high they can go. That notion applies equally well and is rewarded at every bargaining table.

Judge not a man by his answers but by his questions.
– Voltaire

6   Quick is synonymous with risk.

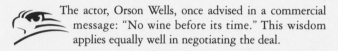 The actor, Orson Wells, once advised in a commercial message: "No wine before its time." This wisdom applies equally well in negotiating the deal.

Optimal negotiators understand that a negotiation is an emotional roller coaster. So, they pace the process. They anticipate (and contribute to) the highs and the lows. From experience, they know that one inevitably follows the other until the ride is over ... until the deal is done.

Agreements realized too early eventually lead to dissatisfaction, for often we reflect later on the feeling that the objective was achieved too easily or too quickly. As has already been noted, the harder we work to reach a mutually acceptable agreement, the greater is our satisfaction with the achievement. And people do need time to get used to new and difficult propositions.

Quality negotiations follow a structured process which, much like a building, requires a plan, the expertise to build and the time to construct. The architect and the builder collaborate with a common purpose in mind. First, there is the foundation. If it is not set firmly in place, the superstructure above (not unlike the negotiating process) will be fragile.

The foundation of a building is as critical to supporting the structure over time as preparation is to a successful negotiation. The remaining elements in the negotiating process likewise require both time and expertise to construct: the opening and the considered exchange of information, the exploration and testing of positions and assumptions, the packaging and

Quick is synonymous with risk.

bargaining of conditions and concessions, and, lastly, the close. All of which, properly executed, requires the right pacing and attention to good time management.

In a negotiation, the proper investment of time brings its just rewards. North Americans, especially, are far too impatient at the bargaining table. We speak and act too quickly. We don't allow deals to ripen and flourish. Not surprisingly, this behaviour is costly. Deals that could be optimized are not. Yet the changes needed to enhance impoverished negotiating outcomes are both minimal and subtle.

Since time is measured in seconds, a pregnant pause at the right moment can be the winning tactic. Through mindful pacing, we can increase the perceived value of the information and concessions we offer. If time changes everything and the ultimate purpose is to change the other person's point of view, then acting hastily is surely counterproductive to achieving better deals.

If you are to persuade, you must appeal
to interest rather than intellect.
– Benjamin Franklin

7   Dumb is better than smart.

Appearing not to know something, especially those things you should know, encourages others to give you useful information. And the dumber you appear to be, the more likely your alter negotiator will offer helpful information and further concessions.

People who appear to be less than competent often end up achieving what they seek largely because we presume they desperately need our help. So we volunteer it freely. Their perceived stupidity engenders our pity and compassion, which prompts a need to attend to their interests at the expense of our own.

Since we aren't really threatened by their behaviour, we let down our guard. Viewing them as incapable of defending themselves, we become as gullible as they appear to be. In the process, we become the unwitting victims of our own efforts to be helpful and caring.

The same principle applies to a negotiation. Whenever you appear unwilling or unable to look after your own best interests, people are more easily persuaded to offer you assistance. Should you ask a series of seemingly dumb questions (and the dumber the better), the other party will often feel compelled to share information he might otherwise conceal.

Conversely, whenever you demonstrate an arrogant, aggressive or know-it-all demeanor, people are less likely to tell you what you need to know or to divulge their real needs and hidden motivations. As a result, you are denied information that may

13

Dumb is better than smart.

prove essential to finding an arrangement that will accommodate the needs of both sides.

Of course, the constancy of the behaviour is critical to its success. If dumb behaviour is only exhibited during negotiations, or done in an exaggerated fashion, the tactic becomes transparent. And thus counterproductive.

Dumb is also relative. "Smart dumb" is asking a lot of seemingly innocent questions while not presuming the answers. Smart dumb is asking the same question after you've already received the answer. When supported by a bewildered, exasperated look, and coupled with extreme tentativeness, the power of the tactic can be profound.

Should your self-concept prevent you from comfortably acting dumb in order to achieve a desired objective, then at least be wary of those negotiators who seem to ask a lot of stupid questions. In a negotiation, there is no such thing as a stupid question.

Smart is when you believe only half of what you hear.
Brilliant is when you know which half.

8 People support what they help to create.

"Either my way or the highway" is an ultimatum destined to fail – even if one of the alternatives offered is genuine and might prove to be beneficial to the other party.

Today, especially, people desire a stake in the decisions they believe may affect their lives. Once they have been given that stake or are otherwise involved in the process, the likelihood that they will follow through on needed actions is enhanced.

Optimal negotiators seek to ensure the other party is a full and willing participant in the negotiating process. With this intent to collaborate comes mutual ownership of the problem and a commitment to finding acceptable solutions. Whenever the problem is perceived to be the other person or his values, a resolution of the issues in dispute becomes more difficult. The wise strategy is the one aimed at encouraging a co-definition of the problem.

Each of us has a fundamental need to be recognized for what we are and know, to be acknowledged (as well as praised) for our ability to contribute to the issue at hand. Good negotiators use that need to their advantage, not only in soliciting new ideas that might prove helpful in resolving the conflict but also in creating an ally for mutual profit improvement. Rather than seeking to impose a solution, the best tactic is to ask for ideas that can either advance the negotiation or provide a platform for your own interests.

A word of caution: never argue or debate the relative merits of your alter negotiator's ideas when they are first presented.

People support what they help to create.

Simply list those with which you disagree in a non-judgmental fashion (both verbally and non-verbally), then move the process forward with an observation such as "That's interesting – do you have any other ideas for dealing with our challenge?"

Never underestimate a person's ability to solve a problem, or to find a solution that might be compatible with your own, if given the opportunity and encouragement to present it. Should you not hear a suggestion that might satisfy your needs, you can always add your own ideas once theirs are exhausted.

You will find that people are more receptive to your solutions after you've listened attentively to theirs. Minimally, you will discover that they will listen better and become less argumentative than is the case when you insist on going first. Remember, people are more likely to act on their own ideas before they accept and act on yours.

If you do believe your best negotiating approach is a "my way or the highway" ultimatum, at least honour this principle by adding this magical phrase: "unless you see it some other way."

The right word may be effective, but no word was ever as effective as the rightly timed pause.
– Mark Twain

9   Planning never ends.

 There is a direct correlation between planning and results. What you do before you begin negotiating will ultimately determine your success.

Preparation is the most important step in the negotiating process. The more time invested in preparing, the less time you will need to negotiate a good deal. Peter Drucker, the acknowledged management guru, has long advised business leaders to "plan your work and work your plan because, if you fail to plan, you plan to fail." The same counsel applies to negotiating.

Planning is more than contemplating and listing one's objectives. In addition to the "whats," it must pay heed to the "hows," or the method and style of negotiating. Planning is organizing information for the purpose of both disguise and discovery, examining key issues and options, assessing your opponent's strengths and weaknesses, evaluating the appropriateness of tactics, and more. Considering the whats of the negotiation without adequate attention to the hows is not planning. It's wishful thinking.

Optimal negotiators thoroughly analyze the situation – both the problem and the opportunity – then examine their leverage and the consequences of the plan not working. Options and alternatives are weighed against the downside risks. Essentials are distinguished from expendables.

Good planning is anticipating surprises by looking beyond the negotiated outcome to the near and the far future and asking a series of "what if" questions. What if the value of money

Planning never ends.

changes? What if the rules and regulations no longer apply? What if this is a bigger success than either of us would ever imagine? Planning is reducing the pressures of bargaining by making perceived issues, threats and concerns explicit. And planning is preparing for objections and resistance by identifying appropriate responses, options and alternatives.

With good planning, risk-taking is more calculated, thereby increasing the odds of success. Preparation also engenders a sense of confidence and control at the bargaining table – and the appearance of control exudes power.

Good preparation enables you to focus on what really matters – to zero in on the questions and answers that can achieve your objectives, to distinguish the wheat from the chaff in what your alter negotiator puts forward for consideration. The better prepared you are, the less you talk, the more you listen and think, and the better your answers become.

If you don't know where you're going, you're likely to end up in a place you don't want to be. You will never regret investing more time (than you think necessary) in planning for your negotiations.

When schemes are laid in advance, it is surprising
how often circumstances fit in with them.
– Sir William Osler

10   The two most critical 5 minutes.

 What you do at the outset of your negotiation will determine the quality of the process. What you do at the end, can determine your success.

The opening minutes of a negotiation should be devoted primarily to establishing rapport and creating a climate conducive to achieving your objectives. People like doing business with people they like. So your initial focus must be to become likeable.

Don't jump right into issues that are divisive or contentious. Attend to social amenities. Ask open-ended questions that enable people to talk about themselves (for, curiously, the more you allow people to discuss themselves, the more they may like you). Make eye contact, nod, smile and listen attentively. Humanize yourself, even if you are representing someone else.

This initial "climate setting" is the necessary first step to achieving collaboration – working together for mutual profit improvement. The quality of this opening encounter is the foundation for the process that follows – so make sure it's stable and worthy of building upon.

The last five minutes of the negotiation are of equal significance. It is essential that you take the time to "agree to what you have agreed." Most negotiators pay insufficient attention to the importance of details at the close of negotiations. They tend to focus on the euphoria of having made the deal rather than ensuring its completeness. As such, they invariably end up renegotiating things that had presumably already been settled.

The two most critical 5 minutes.

Take the time to get all the details. Go beyond the major elements of the transaction. Seek explicit corroboration that your understanding is also hers. In a negotiation, people forget – they do so for tactical reasons or simple convenience or because they have a poor memory. Don't assume the other person will be "good for it." Maybe he will, but maybe he won't.

Why create an irritant in the future relationship when it can be avoided by simply going over the agreement from top to bottom? Eliminate the fuzzies and loose ends, point by point. You'll both be happy you did. Little things can make a big difference in the ongoing satisfaction of both parties.

And beware of nibbling – using the closing moments to ask for "just one more thing." If you nibble, your alter negotiator may be sufficiently irritated to walk away from the deal. If he nibbles, tell him that this is a time for clarification, not further negotiation. Put the pressure where it belongs by asking whether his objective is to reopen the deal and thus "go back to the beginning."

Considering what you will do and what you will say at both of these crucial points in the negotiation can be the difference between winning and losing.

There is a time to win and there is a time to lose.

11 It's only "last and final" when you believe it.

Never make a "last and final" offer and always test the statement when it's used by your alter negotiator.

A "last and final" offer works only when it's accepted at face value and is believed by the other party. Or when the aggravation level is so high that the proposer is prepared to live with the downside risk of having the offer, and thus the deal, rejected. Regardless, it's a high-risk tactic you should avoid. If the proposition is rejected, the proposer has limited options. He can dig a little deeper and lose credibility or face the possibility of deadlock.

Whenever you hear the phrase "last and final," listen closely to the exact words. More often than not, the phrasing that accompanies the ultimatum contains some kind of escape clause – subtle or vague wording that permits the speaker to continue negotiating without losing bargaining leverage. Listen for loopholes and the firmness of consequences and deadlines. Ask yourself what would happen if you didn't agree.

For example, when someone says her offer is last and final because "I can't go any higher," consider the possibility that the real issue is she can't go any higher "at this time" or "without further authorization." Should she say "If you don't take this offer, I'll have to give it to XYZ," does that mean she actually has in hand a competitive bid from XYZ? If "the offer stands for only three days," what happens then?

Do a cost-benefit analysis of the proposal before you. Even though it may be a bluff designed to pressure you into settling

It's only "last and final" when you believe it.

now, have you accomplished all that you set out to achieve? If so, there's no harm in accepting the offer. You have to decide whether you can live with the deal before you or whether the proposition is worth exploring further. A further benefit of testing is the opportunity to gain additional insights into your adversary's bargaining style.

Another option is to buy some time to reflect on the pros and cons of the proposition. "Let me think about it" not only gives the other party time to reflect on the risk inherent in his proposal, it gives you time to think about a creative counter, should that be your intent.

The frequent use of "last and final" offers can be deleterious to your reputation. Remember, it takes two to make a deal. If you accept a "last and final" offer, it's over. If you reject it, preferably with a face-saving alternative, the negotiation is likely to continue.

When you feel you absolutely must have something, you always pay top dollar for it.

12 Questions are windows to the mind.

 In a negotiation, information is the ultimate source of power. And the most important information is that which is purposefully withheld, protected or disguised.

Optimal negotiators understand that it's what they don't know that can hurt them at the bargaining table. They realize that, to win, they must know as much as possible. And the only way to acquire that essential information is through the artful and intelligent use of tactful, probing questions.

An appreciation that questions can be perceived as invasive and thus threatening to one's privacy is critical to asking smart questions – ones that neither offend nor indicate authority or arrogance. Questions should be formulated in an understanding way while serving a strategic function.

In a negotiation, questions must be asked for a purpose. They can be used to get and give information, create focus, establish climate, encourage thinking or bring discussion to an end. Questions can solicit clarification or justification or enable you to change the subject, prompt more information or redirect to another person. While the tactical functions are many, the critical purpose is always to ascertain needs and maintain control. Whoever asks the questions drives the negotiation.

Both timing and phrasing are the keys to successful questioning. The inopportune timing of a question can freeze an opponent into an immovable position. Seek only a limited amount of information at one time – that is, information which can be easily given at that phase of the negotiation. The objective is

Questions are windows to the mind.

to gradually guide the thinking and reasoning of the other party towards answers or conclusions that are conducive to your realizing objectives.

It is always advisable when exploring sensitive issues to remove the perception of threat by explaining the reason for asking your question. A non-forcing question like "How do you feel about this?"permits full and continuing discussion. As long as information is flowing, you are advancing the negotiation.

Tone of voice and tentative phrasing are important. You never want to appear to be aggressive, bullying or arrogant in your knowledge. Try to give the impression that you're just thinking out loud (as opposed to reading from a well rehearsed script or, worse, lecturing).

Since your goal is clarity, avoid assumptions and false inferences. The purpose of opening and accessing windows to the mind is not to impress others with your questioning skill and flair but to gather useful information and ultimately to achieve an understanding and acceptance of your point of view.

The best thing to do when you don't know what to do is to do nothing.

13　Understand your rights.

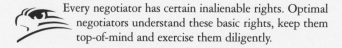Every negotiator has certain inalienable rights. Optimal negotiators understand these basic rights, keep them top-of-mind and exercise them diligently.

Every negotiator has the right to ...

Ask artful, intelligent and probing questions (and listen attentively to the answers given).

Be intentionally slow and dumb at times (or at least somewhat cautious and occasionally even indecisive).

Be wrong (or, at best, more open-minded in considering differing or alternative viewpoints).

Ignore the other person's power advantage (especially when it's used against you in overt, aggressive ways).

Take a break from the negotiation (whenever uncertainty arises or the focus is lost).

Say "I don't really know the answer to that" when you don't know what answer to give (and occasionally when you do).

Not answer the other person's question (and certainly not to feel pressured or obligated to elaborate and embellish on your own answers).

Understand your rights.

Repeat or reframe what you've just said (whenever you're unsure of what to say next).

Walk away from the deal (when either your principles are at stake or to avoid becoming predictable).

Not be too hard on yourself when you lose (because it does and will happen).

Risk is not knowing what you're doing.
— Warren Buffet

14

Change the shape
of the deal.

 No two people will ever have the same needs, information or perceptions. Hence, there is always a way to make a deal.

A story about a legendary Hollywood actress aptly illustrates the point. After starring in an Oscar-winning movie in the forties and realizing she was now a "hot property," she approached her agent with the (then) outrageous request to be paid one million dollars. Given the year, and the industry, this kind of demand from a relatively unknown starlet was unprecedented.

The individual who held her personal services contract was a savvy, highly regarded business executive. On hearing her salary request, his immediate thought was not "how much will she take?" (the normal response of a "numbers negotiator"), but rather "what is she really asking for?" He wanted first to understand the needs behind the number.

Was this starlet's tough opening demand a desire for recognition and peer adulation (which would certainly accompany public knowledge of her success in getting the million dollars)? Did she seek freedom and independence (which would likely follow if her agent was unable meet her seemingly outrageous demand)? Or, was she merely seeking the security of a higher paycheque in a rather precarious profession?

Success in negotiating requires an ability to identify the needs that motivate the expression of numbers. Once discovered, the task is then to change the shape of the deal to accommodate those needs. The million-dollar opening represented her initial "want," not necessarily her ultimate need. The business man

Change the shape of the deal.

was an optimal negotiator. He also knew his client. He was aware she wanted to leave the business for awhile to get married, have children and raise them at home. After which, she aspired to return to her profession. Satisfying her need would have been difficult without a modicum of financial security.

Knowing this, the business man reshaped the deal. He offered her $50,000 a year for 20 years. Was she happy? Delighted. The numbers added up to the sum she sought but the way it was packaged spoke directly to her reason for asking.

What about the business man? Given his financial acumen, he understood the amortization principle and the ravages of inflation on the value of money. His counterproposal cost him far less than the million dollars she initially requested. More importantly, he "tied up" this hot property for at least 20 more years.

This classic win-win outcome was predicated on finding the need that drove the number and then restructuring the deal to enable both parties to achieve their goals. It's a fundamental principle that can work in every negotiation. Don't be intimidated by numbers. Look for needs and creatively seek to satisfy them.

Nothing in the world can take the place of persistence.
— Calvin Coolidge

15   Disguise, don't deceive.

 While at times it may seem easy, necessary or tactically appealing, telling lies in your negotiations can prove to be counterproductive.

Although the statement has an ethical undertone, it is a hard reality that most negotiators learn from painful experience. When you lie, your reputation is at stake. When your reputation is tarnished, your power is diminished. Reputations are formed over time through consistent and reliable performance but can be destroyed in an instant through the thoughtless or careless act of lying.

Deceit is also stressful. When you propose an untruth, the pressure to remember the precise details of your manufactured remark is upon you in every retelling. This stress impairs your ability to be spontaneous and to think of appropriate, tactful responses. And, when all is said and done, never underestimate the other person's ability to detect the incongruence or inconsistency in your voice, body language and even the details of your explanation.

Optimal negotiators are skilled at lie detection. They know that the clues to deceit are easily revealed in facial gestures, eye movements and other nervous gestures. So, lying isn't worth the effort, especially when you understand the principle of disguise.

Disguise acknowledges that correct answers in a negotiation are not necessarily good answers. You are not obligated to reveal information that might put you at a competitive disadvantage. Beyond that truism, the harder you make the other party work

Disguise, don't deceive.

for his answers, the greater will be his satisfaction in receiving them. As important, the harder people work to extract information, the more they will believe the answer to be credible.

Disguise is aided by spontaneity. Preparing disguising responses to difficult questions (the ones you hope will never be asked, but invariably are) is the essence of intelligent negotiating. The perception of the questioner, when confronted by indecision, is that, if you have to think about it, you're probably "making it up."

A good disguising response offers neither precision nor elaboration. It's an answer that doesn't really answer the question asked but that satisfies the questioner. When asked "How long?", a good answer is "Not long." When asked "Why is she selling?", say "Because she's going through a lifestyle change." You've answered the question without giving the reason why, which is what your alter negotiator is seeking. Don't assume you'll get a further probe; answers that don't answer are accepted far more willingly than you might realize.

Process. WOW! What a concept!
— Robin Williams

16   The first number is not the number.

The opening position in a negotiation is never the final position. Naive negotiators open the bargaining process by asking for their "bottom line" and, not surprisingly, rarely get it.

The art of making concessions lies in having sufficient room to negotiate. Optimal negotiators give themselves ample latitude – they start higher than most when selling and lower than most if buying. They creatively broaden the scope of negotiations to ensure they have the room needed to make good trade-offs and enhance mutual profit improvement.

Clearly, the more latitude you give yourself in expressing your opening position the better. Always have a reason for starting where you do. When feasible, open first to create or alter the other party's expectations right from the start – it might influence a better counteroffer.

When your alter negotiator opens, get all his demands, positions and expectations on the table. Don't assume; ask. It might not seem practical but, with experience, you'll discover the power of simple but compelling prompting questions like "Anything else?"

In a study of collective bargaining, where the initial gulf between the parties is normally wide and the willingness to compromise exacerbated by the theatrics of the process, it was discovered that both parties (prior to the start of negotiations) were amenable to conceding more than was necessary to make a deal. There is often a huge disparity between what people say

The first number is not the number.

they want and what they can "live with." In other words, there's invariably more to be had at the bargaining table, provided you know how to construct a negotiating process conducive to acquiring it.

As you read on, you will discover other essential principles that amplify on the strategic importance of the opening position – what you should do, what you should not do, and of what you should be wary. The purpose of the opening number is simply to create new expectations or to change existing assumptions while lowering your alter negotiator's aspiration level.

The opening position is no more than the start of a process and should be treated as such.

Implicit in the phrase "as a general rule"
is that there is always an exception.

17   Make concessions wisely.

Concessions made too quickly produce two undesirable consequences: they whet your alter negotiator's appetite for more and leave you with less to offer when you likely need it most.

In a negotiation, giving gets. You cannot advance your cause or achieve your objectives without providing reciprocal concessions. How you do that will determine your success. What counts is not the magnitude of concessions made but the frequency with which they're given. Give concessions incrementally, with each subsequent offering being a fraction of the prior one, and in a manner that demonstrates a willingness to move negotiations forward. Concessions should send a signal of flexibility, not intransigence.

People rarely appreciate getting something for nothing. So, make the other party work for your concessions. The harder she works, the greater will be her satisfaction with what you eventually provide. And never give something away without getting something in return. Your concessions should be contingent upon theirs: "If you can do that for me, then I can do this for you." Don't feel obligated to respond to their *quid pro quo* proposals. If her proposal is, "Let's split the difference," you can respond, "I can't afford to."

Concessions need not be framed in hard numbers. "I really appreciate your help" and "I'll consider it" will be perceived as concessions. Don't think all or nothing. If you can't get a dinner, get a sandwich. If you can't get a sandwich, get a promise (a concession at a discount rate).

Make concessions wisely.

When asked for a concession, don't be afraid to say "no." Most people are. Saying "no" will make the concessions you have to give seem all the more valued. Don't be ashamed to back away from a concession you've already made but didn't fully understand. It's the final handshake that makes the deal, not the agreements in between.

Think of every concession as real money. Don't lose track of your concessions. Keep a tally of yours and his. A disfavourable scorecard might be worth something – you might even ask for an I.O.U. if the list becomes too one-sided.

Tit-for-tat concessions are unnecessary and unwise (and they create false expectations). If he gives sixty, you can give forty. When you get a concession on price, change the topic to terms. Later, when you return to the price, you can ask for another concession. Conserve your concessions. Later is better than now (because you will need them later). Pause, be tentative and talk about other things. Your hesitation, or your silence, may prompt even further concessions.

The more deeply you listen,
the more eloquently people will speak.

18 Self-control precedes the control of others.

A negotiation is a conflict of interests. And, when vital interests are at stake, emotions are easily aroused. If these emotions remain unchecked, the ability to control the process will be seriously impaired.

We would not need to negotiate if we agreed on everything. Optimal negotiators view conflict as an essential part of the process and are comfortable with it. They realize that the more they can channel their emotions, the more they will think and speak rationally and, thus, the more easily they can control their alter negotiator.

Generally speaking, there are two ways to deal with others in a conflict situation. We can either act rationally or react emotionally. Those who react without thought typically go on the offensive. They attack, criticize and accuse. Their behaviour and their words become exaggerated and intense. This response is usually counterproductive and self-defeating.

Conversely, those who have the presence of mind to stop and think before reacting have a wide variety of strategic options available. Thinking, taking a momentary pause to reflect on what is happening, is the essence of self-control. It is what winning is all about.

On analysis, conflict is an act of co-operation. It is sustained when the antagonists support and energize each other. A thinking response, on the other hand, de-escalates conflict, disarms your adversary and enables you to control the negotiation. Emotionally driven and unthinking negotiators react to tactics

Self-control precedes the control of others.

in accordance with their feelings of the moment. They lose control because they don't know "what's happening." And it shows.

Learn the benefits of "the PCV valve" – Pause, Control, Value. When faced with a confusing or frustrating encounter, take a moment to pause before reacting. Three seconds is a sufficient time-out. When you can do this, you will feel the power of self-control. You are now able to take control of your voice, words and body language.

Your first words should be aimed at valuing the other person. Tell her, "I can understand why you would say that" (because no two people would say the same thing about anything). Understanding the legitimacy of her viewpoint does not compromise yours. But it will make her more receptive to what you have to say. Such are the benefits of self-control in advancing your cause.

Whatever you write on paper should be written as if it will ultimately be read in a court of law.

19   Don't violate the norms.

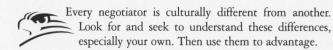 Every negotiator is culturally different from another. Look for and seek to understand these differences, especially your own. Then use them to advantage.

Each of us is the product of a unique set of circumstances. Our cultural experience, and thus our differentiation, includes ethnicity, religion, geography, education, gender and age. This is why the Japanese don't negotiate like the Italians, New Yorkers don't negotiate like Torontonians, men don't negotiate like women, nor children like adults.

Our circumstances and socialization beget different behaviours and different ways of perceiving, reasoning and reacting. They also produce different orientations, understandings and views of what constitutes good negotiating. Which is why cultural stereotypes can provide useful insights into negotiating styles.

Research and practical experience suggest that, at the bargaining table, the Chinese tend to converge on principles but diverge on the specifics. Russians will rarely make unilateral concessions. The French and Italians get emotionally involved. And the Japanese combine their remarkable patience with the strategic use of silence. Contrast these behaviours with typical North American tendencies, like our impatience and willingness to make the first concession, our desire to be reasonable and our inclination toward reciprocity and tit-for-tat concessions.

Beneath this macro-level of bargaining behaviours are negotiating arenas where both the approach and the expectations are quite different and distinctive. Retail negotiating is obviously

Don't violate the norms.

dissimilar from collective bargaining. The tactics and expectations implicit in international diplomacy are not the same as those found in commercial transactions, whether in real estate or corporate mergers.

Differences in negotiating styles can also be observed in the contrasting cultural behaviours of individuals, as exhibited best perhaps in gender differences. An understanding of these dissimilar approaches to negotiating and especially the danger signals inherent in various arenas of bargaining can be critical to your success.

The advice that tells us "When in Rome, do as the Romans do" applies equally well to your negotiations. Understand but don't violate the cultural norms and behavioural expectations of the people with whom you negotiate nor the situations in which you find yourself. Otherwise your tactics will become transparent.

Never get angry. Never make a threat. Reason with people.
— Don Coreleone

20   Be empathic, not chauvinistic.

Without awareness, we are destined to become the victims of our prejudices. We perceive and judge others from that point in the cultural spectrum where we stand rooted. We have a relative, not complete, view of life's transactions, including our negotiations.

When we realize our cherished values represent a very limited view of the cultural universe, we are more likely to accept the opinions and manners of others as being valid. When we can examine our beliefs and actions objectively, we will have more empathy with the thoughts and personalities of others.

What if the Japanese could discard their ultra-politeness? If the French were to eschew their sense of intellectual superiority, and the Germans realize their cult of efficiency may be counter-productive at times? What if North Americans could be less insensitive, less dollar-minded, less pragmatic and could tone down their well-meant bluntness and excessive informality?

Chauvinism is seeing our cultural traits as superior; empathy is accepting our differences and building on them in a positive manner. The attributes for achieving empathy in negotiations are tact, humour, sensitivity, flexibility, compromise, politeness, and patience. Empathic negotiators are skilled at clarifying objectives, attentive listening, respecting confidentiality, inspiring trust and, above all, constantly striving to see things from the other's point of view.

While we cannot exist without some degree of cultural stereo-typing – because it provides a useful point of reference in

Be empathic, not chauvinistic.

determining the appropriateness of our behaviour towards strangers – we must learn to accept and manage these stereo-types. We must appreciate the positive values we perceive in others while minimizing or perhaps even laughing off (if we can) what we see as conflicting beliefs.

Conflict and stress, a necessary part of the negotiating process, give rise to excessive stereotyping while reinforcing our own cultural biases. The antidote is to seek to embrace the negoti-ating advantage inherent in an appreciation of cultural diversity.

Self-criticism, a more accurate understanding of cultural strengths and weaknesses, the honing of one's ability to give appropriate and tactful responses, and practicing adaptive behaviours without sacrificing one's integrity are skills to be drawn on when cultures collide at the negotiating table. These are the behaviours, attributes and skill sets of the optimal negotiator.

You can't sell them if you don't speak their language.

21 Cultural strengths can be weaknesses.

 The attributes that distinguish us from another can be negotiating liabilities, especially if we fail to understand the impact of our behaviours.

While Scots tend to view stubbornness as a positive trait, flexible Italians see intransigence and the more diplomatic English observe a lack of artfulness. The Japanese may discover one day that when they say 'yes' at the bargaining table, the rest of the world does not know they likely mean 'no.' Spaniards are apt to view the Swiss as stuffy and excessively law-abiding. Italians invariably find Norwegians to be gloomy. Argentinians are generally considered conceited by other South Americans. The Germans think Australians are undisciplined. The Japanese tend to see straight-talking Americans as rude.

How are we viewed by the rest of the world? What ingrained cultural limitations and biases make North Americans "weak" negotiators? Our cultural tendencies, if unchecked can produce major flaws in negotiating skill sets. For example, we frequently let our egos get in the way of our objectives. We view negotiations as a way of scoring points rather than satisfying needs. We are overly impatient; we don't allow opportunities to ripen. We push when we should wait. Time, not patience, is viewed as money.

North American negotiators are invariably far too rational and analytical. We detest silence. We have an inordinate respect for deadlines. We have a need to know and are more comfortable with certainty than with ambiguity. We are reciprocity (compromise) oriented. And we have a strong need to be liked (perhaps the most vulnerable kind of negotiator is the

Cultural strengths can be weaknesses.

one who seeks the approval of others). In a context other than negotiating, many of these characteristics would probably be considered strengths.

As always, be wary of cultural generalizations. They are intended to generate insights, not definitive conclusions. North America is a big place. There are cultures within cultures. Just as Albertans don't bargain like Ontarians, New Yorkers don't negotiate like Californians. Compared to Canadians, Americans are generally more individualistic, ethnocentric, boastful, reckless, nationalistic, less tolerant and jump to conclusions more quickly. Compared to Americans, Canadians are moderately cautious and low key, conservative, typically more worldly and sensitive to multi-cultural differences, more trusting and have a tendency to understate things.

The more we know about our cultural biases and our personal preferences, the better equipped we are to address our negotiating weaknesses and turn them into strengths.

Speak softly and carry a big stick.
Don't mumble. And don't swing the stick.

22 Know your adversary's needs.

Beyond a knowledge of the dynamics of human behaviour, successful negotiating requires an ability to understand the unique personality and motivations of the person who opposes you.

No matter how bizarre or absurd the other person's behaviour may seem to you, it always makes sense to him. Every negotiator has his own self-concept, ego strength and aspiration level. Every negotiator possesses his own idea of what fair and reasonable mean. Every negotiator has a different, unique set of needs that she alone believes are important. Never assume that what's fair or important to you is likewise fair or important to him.

Although we may have similar needs, we are differentiated from one another by the degree of importance we place upon our own needs and interests. The needs we hold in common range from basic survival to social and ego needs. And our fundamental purpose in life, and therefore also in our negotiations, is to satisfy those needs.

Maslow states that we have a hierarchy of needs. Our basic needs are for survival and pain-avoidance, like the need for order and predictability, freedom from surprises, avoiding a loss, safety and security, help in time of crisis and freedom from fear and anxiety. Our social needs are for acceptance and belonging, recognition and approval, participation, friendship, and appreciation. Ego needs include the need for uniqueness, independence, self-expression, privacy, self-determination, dominance, achievement, growth, self-esteem and status.

Know your adversary's needs.

Optimal negotiators seek to discover and understand the need that drives the number, which is articulated at the outset of the process as a "want." They don't play "the numbers game" that invariably produces a result somewhere near the middle. Instead, they endeavour to optimize the numbers for both parties by identifying, creatively acknowledging and satisfying their adversary's unique needs. This in no way diminishes their pursuit of self-interest simply because no two people will ever have identical needs.

To reach an optimal deal, you must learn as much as you can about the person with whom you're negotiating. Is she seeking money or a feeling of power? Is it a desire to avoid risk? Achieve financial stability? Peace of mind? Praise? To be thought of as fair and nice? To be treated with dignity? To avoid unpleasant surprises? To receive help in making a tough decision? Seeing her idea recognized? Stability in the relationship? A good explanation? Affiliation with you?

The list of needs that reflect the uniqueness of each negotiator's personality is practically endless. So too then is the opportunity to negotiate a both-win deal.

People are usually more convinced by reasons they discovered
than by those found by others.
— Blaise Pascal

23 Know yourself better.

The more you understand your own needs, interests, motivations, aspirations, weaknesses and biases, the more effective and successful you will be at the negotiating table.

Self-knowledge requires an awareness of our hot buttons, prejudices and vulnerabilities – those emotional "soft spots" that trigger our anger, frustration, confusion, anxiety, fear as well as other unproductive feelings that lead to unthinking responses. As we come to appreciate and understand ourselves better, we move closer to developing a hot-button immune system.

To know thyself is to discover your pause button, a state of mind that enables you to create emotional distance from those who choose to attack your character and your convictions. When you are able to consciously achieve that mental "time out," you will not be victimized by tactics aimed at demeaning your self-image and self-worth.

How can you get to know yourself better? By answering some questions aimed at revealing your weaknesses and biases and doing so as honestly as possible. Questions like: Why do some people annoy me? What are my personal limitations and what can I do to correct them? What are my personal strengths and how can I use them more fully? What are my prejudices and stereotypes (that lead me to prejudge people without evidence)? What are my pet peeves and sacred cows?

There are others. Where am I vulnerable emotionally? Does ego-inflating behaviour make me a willing victim? What don't

Know yourself better.

I like about myself and is this reality-based? To what extent, and why, do I have the respect of colleagues? What am I really seeking from others? This frank introspection will enable you to recognize and accept your assumptions, stereotypes and hot buttons.

Self-knowledge requires a critical look in the mirror. True self-analysis is finding honest answers to some tough questions that can enable you to become less vulnerable to those whose primary intent is to use your perceived self-worth as a tactic against you. Self-knowledge requires you to use experience as a teacher, learning invaluable lessons from past mistakes. Discerned learning strengthens your character and enables you to make better strategic choices under pressure.

The more self-understanding you possess, the greater is your freedom in searching for and finding valuable insights into your opponent's negotiating psyche, motivations and interests.

The unexamined life is not worth living.
— Socrates

24   Winning can also mean losing.

 When the quality of the relationship is the issue or when dealing with important people in your life who have less power than you, take the long-term view.

Optimal negotiators see negotiating as an ongoing process, where outcomes set up new beginnings. Consider marriage. When you first meet the person with whom you might spend the rest of your life, you embark upon a process of continuous negotiation. There will be many isolated events, some trivial, some momentous. But the outcome of any single event is the precursor of the one that will inevitably follow. Success in the latter will be influenced by your performance in the former. Residual feelings will be carried forward.

Knowing what's important and when to relent or concede to your partner's wants is critical to the quality of the relationship. Perhaps traditional marriage vows should be revised to contain the phrase "Love, honour and ... negotiate."

A process orientation to negotiating puts the focus on what's right for the relationship, not what's comfortable or convenient for one party at the moment. The true needs of both parties are considered paramount, not their conflicting expression of interests and wants. It also means focusing on future possibilities. What can be and will be takes priority over what is or was.

The challenge experienced by most people in dealing with others is that they are primarily event focussed, not process focussed. Those who understand this difference realize that win-win requires a longer-term view and a creative search for

Winning can also mean losing.

mutual profit improvement. Win-lose, conversely, is taking a shorter-term perspective. In which case, the objective becomes winning at the expense of the other person and, typically, at the expense of the relationship. Win-lose is short-term gain in exchange for long-term pain.

Unfortunately, win-lose is too often an instinctive response, especially when we perceive bullying or insensitive behaviour in others. In such circumstances, our natural defence is to react by "shooting from the lip" without any thought of the consequences. Accordingly, we only succeed in energizing, if not legitimizing, the behaviour of our adversary.

Any fool can be a win-lose negotiator. View negotiating as a process, not an event. Take the long-term view and enrich your significant relationships. Therein lies the wisdom that says losing can sometimes be winning.

To give a reason for anything is to breed a doubt of it.
— William Hazlit

25 Build acceptance through pacing.

Just as a hypnotist can create a state of intensified receptiveness and suggestibility in a subject, optimal negotiators establish trust, alignment, rapport and, ultimately, acceptance through deliberate pacing.

Pacing is using statements and gestures that mirror the other person's words and behaviours. The simplest form is known as descriptive pacing, in which the seller formulates accurate, if banal, descriptions of the buyer's observations and experiences. The purpose is to engender an almost unconscious affinity between the negotiators as a foundation for encouraging agreement. As an example, "You're thinking this could be a wise investment, Sheila," connects with and subtly influences the alter negotiator's thought process in a personal way.

In objection pacing, the seller agrees with the buyer's objection, thus matching his remarks to those of the buyer. From that position of seeming agreement, the seller craftily leads the customer to a position that negates or undermines the objection. "I agree that it's a lot of money ... perhaps we can restructure the payment plan to better accommodate your needs." Done well, pacing has more to do with how something is said than with what is said.

With an almost hypnotic effect, the negotiator seeks to mirror the voice tone, rhythm, volume, and speech rate of the other person. She also matches the other's posture, body language, and mood. She tactfully adopts some of her adversary's characteristic verbal language. If the buyer is slightly depressed, the negotiator empathizes and acknowledges that she too has been

Build acceptance through pacing.

feeling "a little down" lately. The objective is to become a biofeedback mechanism, effectively sharing and reflecting the other person's reality.

Once a bond of trust and rapport is created, the skilled negotiator begins to add suggestions and indirect commands that will persuade the other to change his point of view. A subtle but effective technique is to embed a command into a seemingly innocuous statement – "A good investor knows how to make a quick decision, John."

As you pronounce these commands, slow your speech, look the buyer directly in the eyes, and say each word forcefully. The placement of a person's name in a sentence can make a significant difference in how strongly the sentence influences the listener. Names give commands extra impact.

Information that, by itself, might be rejected takes on a powerful human dimension and force when its presentation incorporates the principles of pacing.

Chance favours only the prepared mind.
– Louis Pasteur

26   The eyes reveal lies.

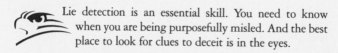 Lie detection is an essential skill. You need to know when you are being purposefully misled. And the best place to look for clues to deceit is in the eyes.

Most people are not very good at identifying lies. Yet the ability to do so is more science than art. Research suggests that certain body language gestures provide better clues to deceptive behaviours than others. In particular, look for mixed messages and discrepancies between the verbal and non-verbal channels of communication (*e.g.*, a smiling face with an angry voice). While actors are trained to do it well, it is difficult for most people to control these channels simultaneously. Communication discrepancies are typical in sarcasm and humour, which are intended. But discrepancies revealed during the telling of a lie are unintentional and thus more easily detected.

The ability to deceive varies with the sending capacity of the channel (the face, body or voice) communicating the lie. The face has maximal sending capacity and is especially well-equipped to tell lies. By contrast, the body is less consciously controllable, especially under stress. While body movements, such as fidgeting or other signs of nervousness, often betray deceit, research indicates that voice pitch is a more dependable indicator than facial expression. For some, the ears may be better than the eyes at distinguishing truth from falsehood.

Gender is a factor in the ability to detect lies. Women are generally better than men at reading non-verbal messages. But the advantage decreases steadily when presented with more deceptive channels, like hand gestures and tone of voice. As

The eyes reveal lies.

communication becomes more fraudulent, a man's accuracy in detecting lies improves relative to a woman's.

Eye movement is a telltale signal of lying. The eyes move, sometimes almost imperceptibly, whenever we have to concentrate and particularly when we are required to access information stored in memory. This is because the optic nerves are "wired" directly to the brain. Curiously, this neural connection is made to the opposite hemisphere of the brain and, depending upon which brain function is engaged (either information is being recalled from memory or it is being created for fraudulent purposes), research tells us that deception or truth can be revealed.

Beyond your own natural instincts for detecting lies, there is an impressive body of literature on the subject that awaits your investigation. It is a knowledge that can lessen your chances of becoming a victim.

The meek shall inherit the earth but not its mineral rights.
— J. Paul Getty

27   Gain credibility through disclosure.

While a negotiator's success is predicated largely on the ability to disguise and protect information, disclosure can be a useful tactic for building trust and eliciting important information.

If ever you've had a airline flight of several hours duration in the presence of a seat mate who "likes to talk," you are familiar with the power of disclosure. It begins with casual conversation and innocuous small talk and, over time, proceeds to delve into far more personal matters. It can become an unwitting competition over who can reveal the most. When the flight has finally ended (unless business cards are exchanged), you disembark the plane without even having learned the other's name. Yet, in the course of the discussion, you likely ascertained intimate details about his family life, where he went to school, his favourite pastimes, his business and associated problems.

Similarly, in a negotiation, disclosure usually begets disclosure. The more information we reveal about ourselves, the greater the likelihood the other party will reciprocate. And, the more we know about one another, the greater the likelihood we will discover mutual interests and find common ground.

Disclosure can also add credibility to your message. We make ourselves, and the position we want to convey, more believable when we reveal information to which others are not necessarily entitled. By disclosing, we take others into our confidence and this, more often than not, prompts them to behave in a like manner. It is an unthinking response, a manifestation of a need to be accepted by others.

Gain credibility through disclosure.

Disclosure is even more powerful when the information we choose to reveal is that which we would only divulge in the presence of a close personal friend, someone we implicitly trust.

While the giving of such information is often inadvisable, it serves as an ulterior motive when it is perceived as placing the other negotiator at a slight competitive advantage *vis-a-vis* your interests. When it is viewed in that way, the probability of reciprocity is even greater.

As with all the advice offered in these pages, always maintain perspective. Giving away too much information that might otherwise be logically protected or disguised, or doing so in a frivolous and reckless fashion, will engender suspicion and caution in the other person. And that will be of no benefit.

If you think you can or can't, you're always right.
— Henry Ford I

28 Conflict and tension are essential ingredients.

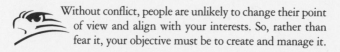 Without conflict, people are unlikely to change their point of view and align with your interests. So, rather than fear it, your objective must be to create and manage it.

Conflict is an inevitable and necessary part of the negotiating process. Tactics are stress-inducing devices that prompt people to reconsider their demands and let go of their wants. Discovery, learning, change, progress and even co-operation are more likely to occur in a climate of engineered conflict aimed at stimulating involvement and generating creativity.

Conflict has both negative and positive functions. The dysfunctional consequences are many. Destructive conflict can produce psychological damage – people don't feel good about themselves when forced to act as antagonists. Conflict can also create a level of distrust that diminishes the quality of information which is so necessary to reaching both-win outcomes.

In conflict situations, the desire to cooperate decreases and defensiveness – intense, exaggerated and repetitious behaviour – increases. The incidence of perceptual barriers which impair our ability to understand rises. To compound this problem, we fail to "stop and think" and, thus, often react inappropriately.

Most of us are keenly aware of these negative consequences but fail to appreciate that conflict can also serve as a powerful force for positive outcomes. When tension is present, often the real issues and concerns are clarified and hidden problems come to the surface where they can be acknowledged, openly discussed and resolved. How often have you heard it said: "Well, that's

Conflict and tension are essential ingredients.

fine for you to say, but what about six months ago when ...." In an atmosphere of conflict, the real issue, the one that has been festering below the surface for one party but forgotten or ignored by the other, can be addressed.

Without a degree of tension, there is little impetus to be creative. A common attribute of creative genius is the existence of adversity that strengthens character. Likewise, in a negotiation, creative problem solving inevitably flows from conflict. The issue is neither capitulation nor concession but, rather, the creation of inventive "third options" that address the needs of both sides.

People learn, let go of precious assumptions and change their point of view when they are appropriately challenged. Human nature suggests that most people would rather avoid a problem than put in the time and effort to solve it. All these good things become possible when conflict is introduced but managed with a purpose in mind.

Unreality is the true source of powerlessness.
What we do not understand, we cannot control.
— Charles Reich

29   Build power incrementally.

 Without power, you cannot win. And, since power depends largely upon perception, the optimal negotiator manages this perception by building his power gradually.

The strategic accumulation, management and use of one's power must acknowledge certain basic principles. The first is that power exists only to the extent that it is perceived and accepted by the other party.

Some people are simply less willing to be controlled or dominated by others. They would rather do without than be exploited by pressure tactics at the bargaining table. For these people, aggressive, dramatic and forceful tactics only result in defensiveness, rigidity and perceptual distortion. Be aware of how others respond to your power, both real and perceived.

The exercise of power always entails costs and risks. An analysis of the consequences of failure, especially in the use of certain pressure tactics, is a necessary consideration for all negotiators. The objective is not ego gratification by ensuring they see you as a powerful or superb tactician but rather the making of deals that support your needs and accommodate your objectives.

The amount of power exercised must be proportional to what is warranted. If the use of power is overly aggressive and therefore perceived to be disproportionate to what the situation warrants, or what the other person can tolerate, he may react in an "adrenal" or emotional fashion. This generates unpredictable behaviours and hence unnecessary risk.

Build power incrementally.

Power is best applied in negotiating when it is either implied or manifested without action of any kind. An opponent who senses or believes you have power, or that some action can and might be taken against her, will react accordingly.

While power is to be exercised in a thoughtful if not calculated way, its expression is always limited. The scope, range and impact of your power are dependent upon many factors, such as the other person's strength, position or role, the situation at hand, the effect of relevant policy and regulations, a recognition of ethical and professional standards, the existence of present or future competition, as well as the other party's preparedness, options and alternatives.

Use your power intelligently and with care. Despite the temptation at times, it is not a blunt instrument designed to bludgeon your opponent. Its use should always be tactful, appropriate and aimed at achieving your goal without incurring negative consequences.

All power is based on perception.
— Herb Cohen

30

Define the reason for "no."

People say "no" for a reason. Rather than debating their resistance or objections, seek to discover the reason behind the "no" and then offer creative alternatives for their consideration.

Negotiating is fundamentally a problem solving process, a structured exercise consisting minimally of five steps. The first is to define the problem (that creates the resistance). Seen in this context, "no" is just another way of saying "I have a problem with that." Unless and until you know the nature, dimensions and scope of the obstacle that separates you from realizing your needs, you cannot help either party move toward common ground. Rather than energizing reservations and entrenchment, begin by asking a series of questions that enable you to comprehend the reason(s) that prevent him from saying "yes" to your proposal.

The second step is to generate ideas – potential and alternative solutions to the disagreement. Since everyone sees things differently, it's likely you both have different ways of addressing the issues at hand. Synergy is combining your ideas and suggestions with theirs. At this stage of problem solving, you neither justify nor debate the ideas. You just list them as possibilities for consideration.

Next, mutually select an idea (for further discussion) that might address the seemingly divergent needs of both parties. See how far you've come? You're no longer fighting his "no," you're now talking about the feasibility or efficacy of alternative approaches to overcoming the challenge that divides you. The remaining

Define the reason for "no."

steps in the process are implementation and monitoring, both of which will occur after the negotiation ends (and which may also provide further opportunities to negotiate).

Discovering the reason behind the "no" advances the discussion to proposing and evaluating creative alternatives. When you identify the one that has both merit and mutual benefits, be sure the essential details – how, when, the cost and other pertinent factors relating to implementation – are adequately covered off.

Whenever you hear "no" in a negotiation, listen to the exact words that accompany it and observe the non-verbal support. Often the phrasing will reveal a lack of firmness or otherwise indicate some room to manoeuvre.

Resist the natural tendency to react by arguing, getting tough or aggressive or, worse, withdrawing. "No" is an emotional trigger. Remind yourself that differences of opinion are normal and that "no" is neither absolute nor final, unless you make it so.

If you can't fight it, study it.

31   Time changes everything.

 The success of tactics varies in direct proportion to the amount of time invested in their execution. Much like green bananas, tactics need time to ripen and be fruitful.

Too often, our impatience causes us to rush the process. This impairs our chances of winning. In a negotiation, a little bit of patience is more than a virtue; it can be money in the bank.

Although we are socially predisposed towards impatience, we need to remind ourselves that time is measured in seconds as well as in hours and days. A few seconds, a pregnant pause, may be more than sufficient to change the other person's perception of the firmness of your position, especially if you are known to act hastily or otherwise appear in a hurry to complete the transaction.

Take, for example, the question: "Is that your best price?" It is, most assuredly, a good question to ask in any negotiation. But the question becomes all the more powerful, and the ensuing results will most assuredly be greater, when it is asked at the end of the conversation rather than at the beginning.

After a period of time has passed, the question becomes more than an apparent attempt to gauge perceived value. It stimulates the perception of risk. Your alter negotiator may now believe that, should he not provide a concession at this critical juncture of the negotiation, his investment of time thus far may prove to be for naught. Good timing (of both questions and tactics) induces better concessions.

Time changes everything.

Likewise, the more time people are given to think and talk about difficult situations or propositions, the more comfortable they will become in understanding and accepting them.

Reflecting upon and then rationalizing the pros and cons of accepting a tough proposal or conceding on one's initial position requires time. We need that time to become more familiar, if not comfortable, with the idea or request, perhaps by talking to friends or just "sleeping on it" before we are able to eventually accept, endorse and embrace it.

Optimal negotiators view time as their ally and patience as power. Horace Bushnell once observed that: "It is not necessary for all men to be great in action. The greatest and sublimest power is often simple patience." His advice has direct and profound application at the bargaining table.

The meaning is the metamessage.
– Deborah Tannen

32 Alter your communication ratios.

Negotiating is fundamentally an act of communication that places a premium on artful questioning, attentive listening and deciphering unintended verbal cues and non-verbal gestures.

Information is the ultimate source of power at the bargaining table. You obtain it by asking thoughtful and probing questions, listening carefully to the answers and understanding the hidden or feigned meanings that are inherent in the process of negotiating. You unintentionally give it away by answering too freely, without adequate prior thought, or by revealing your motives through habitual gestures and behavioural responses.

Our effectiveness is a direct consequence of the degree to which we choose to do things one way or another. We can define this relationship between contrasting actions in terms of a ratio. A 50:50 ratio implies an even split; something that we do equally well and poorly. Decision making, for example, involves a split between rational and emotional thinking. The act of communicating can be viewed as a ratio between speaking and listening. Optimal negotiators deliberately skew that ratio in their favour by listening more than speaking.

When we communicate, we typically talk and listen, ask and answer questions, take note of (or are oblivious to) body language and meta-talk. For communication to occur, we must do all these things. We do not operate exclusively on one side or the other of this communication ratio. We both give and get information. But the extent to which we are aware of the need to alter this ratio toward the gathering of pertinent and

Alter your communication ratios.

meaningful information is the extent to which we become more powerful negotiators.

A winning negotiator knowingly endeavours to ask more probing and intelligent questions than does the other party. She listens more and talks less, and she listens with patience and discipline. She knows that the more deeply she listens, the more eloquently others will speak.

While most people pay little attention to non-verbal signals, she is mindful of their importance in revealing useful information and therefore also focussed and observant. She seeks to interpret the potentially hidden meanings in cavalier or seemingly innocent remarks and she looks intently for telltale gestures that help to clarify contradictory statements.

Poor negotiators are unaware of the need to consciously skew the communication ratio to their advantage. Optimal negotiators focus their time, attention and skill more on the questioning, listening and interpreting side of the equation. They resist the temptation to give away too much information or take the other person's behaviour too literally.

Taking calculated risks is quite different from being rash.
— George S. Patton

33 Proposals advance negotiations.

You cannot win a negotiation by arguing. The expression of hard line, seemingly unassailable facts and intransigent positions will only entrench opposing points of view and make constructive dialogue more difficult.

Optimal negotiators never press their point in an intense, exaggerated fashion; rather, they make proposals and suggestions. Their purpose is to encourage open-mindedness and the creation of possibilities, to discover what the alter negotiator values about the issues under discussion and to ascertain common ground and convergent interests that enable the negotiation to move forward to a mutually profitable conclusion.

Optimal negotiators know the difference between a want and a need. They appreciate that people are more likely to act on their own ideas before accepting theirs. They probe and explore to discover which creative proposition, alternative, or "supposal" might strike a responsive chord with the other party. Their objective is to engender collaboration and problem solving.

A proposal is neither a statement of firm intent nor a commitment that obligates its author. Rather, it's an invitation to discuss and explore possibilities. Its primary purpose is to enable you to gauge "what it's worth" to the other negotiator. That knowledge equips you to frame appealing suggestions – hypothetical propositions that might form the basis of more concrete offers while stimulating meaningful counter-proposals and continuing dialogue between the parties.

When negotiators are able to discuss and debate the merits of differing alternatives long enough, without rancor, threat or

Proposals advance negotiations.

defensiveness, they invariably find convergent ground and mutual advantage. In many cases, this area of potential agreement represents a "third option," one that neither party proposed but that both contributed to creating.

The phrasing of proposals is critical to their acceptance. Focusing your suggestions on divisive issues, contentious problems or divergent grievances only produces a rush to defensiveness, criticism or rejection. This is not a climate conducive to finding both-win ideas.

Optimal negotiators seek to engineer supportive negotiating climates where the purpose is to build on ideas, not tear them down. In such climates, the incidence of deal making is higher and the quality of negotiations considerably better. Proposals that contain explicit reference to possible solutions and workable remedies will invariably generate a mutually supportive and collaborative negotiating environment.

Argument that does not contain credible new information will be seen as self-serving and consequently ineffectual.
— Jeanne M. Brett

34   Power is perceived.

Power at the negotiating table is not what you possess but what your opponent thinks you possess.

Power flows largely from your beliefs and self-concept. If you genuinely believe you are powerful, you will act accordingly. Conversely, if you think you don't have power, even though you do, then you will not demonstrate it.

When you believe wholeheartedly in your competence and talents, you will be perceived as a powerful person. If you have a strong sense of your own self-worth, others will see the power of your self-esteem in your actions and hear it in your words. If you think you are capable of becoming an optimal negotiator, you will become one.

In every relationship, there exists an imbalance of power. There are no exceptions to this fundamental principle. Though we might assume that, in a healthy relationship, both parties are equally powerful, that is never the case. Power is neither mutually distributed nor is it static. Depending on the individuals, the situation and the circumstances, power is dynamic and fluid. In a strong, resilient relationship, such as a marriage, power is constantly shifting between the partners. In certain situations, one party will possess more power than the other. This dynamic disequilibrium leads to mutual admiration, respect and love that, over time, serves to bind the relationship.

It is helpful to view the distribution of power as an equation. Understanding the changing nature of this equation and managing it to advantage will ultimately mean success. In

Power is perceived.

win-win negotiations, a key objective is to diminish your power in the eyes of the other person, especially when he has less power than you. Being perceived as an equal encourages a climate of collaboration and stimulates both-win thinking.

When people lose in a negotiation to someone they perceive as having more power, they inevitably rationalize the outcome as a consequence of the power imbalance, rather than the merits given or their ability to creatively resolve the differences. When that happens, they eventually seek out opportunities to even up the score.

Power distorts communication. Making conscious efforts, albeit tactically, to balance the equation by removing the implied threat of your power greatly improves the quality of the discussion and encourages an evaluation and acceptance of your point of view.

In win-lose encounters, your purpose should be clear – focus on making your power advantage explicit and on ensuring the other party believes you have more power than you actually possess.

A thing is important if anyone think it important.
– William James

35 More things are negotiable than we realize.

 Negotiating is a generic life skill. In virtually everything we do, and with almost everyone we meet, we have an opportunity to negotiate.

The art of negotiating is knowing how to satisfy your needs and resolve differences. It is a process of finite principles but infinite variables. It requires a knowledge of human behaviour, power, creativity and communication. It is a delicate mixture of psychology and philosophy, of art and science, of style and substance. It rewards intuition and gut instinct as highly as intellect and it prizes common sense as much as genius.

In some arenas, such as retail and commercial transactions, collective bargaining and international diplomacy, negotiating is a given. In other situations, it may not seem as obvious. Yet whenever we seek to achieve personal or professional goals, exchange ideas, change attitudes, influence decisions, reach an agreement or seek to enhance the quality of our relationships, we are (or should be) negotiating.

If negotiating is the ability to persuade and convince others, there is no comparable skill that can immeasurably enhance the quality of your personal and professional life. Whether we are buying, selling, managing, persuading superiors, motivating subordinates, nurturing parent-child and spousal relationships, or making complex corporate deals, we are negotiating.

Restricting your concept of negotiating to getting a better price, measured in dollars and cents, is limiting your possibilities for personal growth and success. Surely anything that is the

More things are negotiable than we realize.

product of a negotiation must also, by definition, be negotiable.

Even seemingly inviolate laws are often negotiated, as evidenced by the incidence of plea bargaining. And why not? These laws were initially created through a process of "negotiation" by parties of interest, like lobbyists and politicians, who were convinced to promulgate what they believed to be acceptable codes of conduct.

Yet unforeseen factors often come into play which create opportunities for further negotiating – such as the certainty of the conviction, the trade-off in offering up a more dastardly perpetrator, or the cost of litigation, and so on. Life always provides the circumstances and alternatives that ultimately give rise to negotiating as an efficient and satisfactory way of resolving issues and making better deals.

The only thing that is not negotiable is that which you refuse to negotiate. It takes more than knowledge, power and creativity to negotiate. It requires a willingness to do it. Many understand intellectually how to negotiate but few are motivated to do it well.

Let us never negotiate out of fear,
but let us never fear to negotiate. .
– John F. Kennedy

36 Every negotiation has the same fundamental purpose.

The purpose of a negotiation is to change the other person's point of view about you, your motives and the issues being discussed. Until you can do that, your objectives cannot be realized.

Most people wrongly assume that the primary purpose of negotiations is to achieve agreements, solve problems, satisfy needs, resolve conflicts or get better deals. These may be the ultimate objectives. But they can only be achieved when your alter negotiator changes his perception, and then his understanding, of why you're doing what you're doing at that moment in time. Only when that happens is he more likely to understand your position and align with your interests.

This distinction is not academic; it is critical to increasing your winning percentage. Your success in life is a function of where you choose to focus your attention and thus your efforts. That principle applies to everything you do, including your negotiations. Focus your efforts on getting people to change their viewpoint and success will likely follow.

Negotiations consist of both content (the "what") and process (the "how"). While both are important, the latter is critical to realizing your objectives. A content-focus inevitably, over time, becomes confrontational while a process-orientation seeks to engender collaboration. Winning lies in creating the optimal mix of these two opposing styles relative to the various stages of the negotiation and the appropriate climate for achieving the desired outcome.

Every negotiation has the same purpose.

If you are suspicious of my motives, you will not accept, understand or embrace what I want to tell you. Therefore, it would be wise for me to concentrate on the process, or how I conduct myself during the negotiation, in an effort to reduce your concerns. By soliciting your trust, for example, I can encourage you to tell me what I need to know to make a good deal (either for me or for both of us).

When the process is perceived to be neither threatening nor intimidating, you are more likely to give me quality information and thereby enhance my power. In such a climate, I am better able to influence your point of view regarding my intentions and thus the chance of achieving my ultimate objective is vastly improved.

The most efficacious vehicle I can use to enable you to see me in a more positive light, and reduce your apprehension and presumption of ulterior motives, is to seek to understand and then appear to align with your needs. Since your needs are not the same as mine, this is not as difficult as it might seem.

The law of the harvest governs.
We will always reap what we sow — no more, no less.

37   Open realistically.

You never get a second chance to make a first impression. The same advice applies to your opening position at the bargaining table. The higher you open, the better the deal.

When it comes to negotiating, most North Americans are far too reasonable. In contemplating their tactical options, they worry too much about what the other party may be thinking about the perceived "fairness" of their opening. This unfounded concern invariably affects the quantum and firmness of their initial position. They become overly preoccupied with the fear that their number might be seen as too high or too low, thus eliciting a perception that they are unreasonable or motivated by greed. This ill-founded assumption limits the potential for optimal results.

A reasonable opening, by definition, factors in past performance and comparable situations (in other words, what might be "reasonably" expected under similar circumstances) and then adds an incremental margin to the initial number as the necessary room to negotiate.

A realistic opening, on the other hand, acknowledges the fundamental purpose of the negotiating process – to create new expectations and provide ample room within which to maneuver creatively. The greater your latitude between opening and objective, the less your stress, the better your decision making and the greater the potential for outstanding deals. A realistic opening helps you to test, challenge and explore.

Open realistically.

If, for example, you seek a price of $50, a reasonable opening might be $60. A realistic opening, however, one that satisfies the criteria above, would be $70. At $60, your buyer is already thinking of a settlement lower than that amount; at $70, however, he's anticipating a higher settlement (all because of where you started). A margin of $20 provides more room to move (and is thus less stressful) than does one of $10. Admittedly, market or competitive circumstances might prevail and constrain your opening but your primary purpose in putting forward this initial position is to alter or undermine his expectations.

Always support your opening position with a reason. If you can substantiate your number, regardless of the reason, it's not excessive. People may disagree with it but they can't disagree with your rationale. It is, after all, yours. Never assume your opening will be laughed off or ridiculed. That is the fear that makes us shy away from realistic openings.

While unlikely, should you ever hear an "Are you crazy?" response to your opening, there is an appropriate counter. Maintain your composure. Simply say, "No, I'm not crazy. We're negotiating. That's my opening position. What's yours?" This is an answer that will calm your fear and also one you may never have to use.

> *I'm a slow walker, but I never walk backwards.*
> *— Abraham Lincoln*

38   Giving gets.

Without reciprocal risk and mutual movement, deals cannot be made. To get what you seek, you must give something that satisfies the other side in order to induce them to do likewise.

The expectation of reciprocity is cultural. Just as we usually don't expect to receive something for nothing, it's also foolish to anticipate concessions without offering some in kind as either incentive or compensation. As always, this must be done artfully to minimize your costs.

What counts is the frequency of one's concessions, not the magnitude. Offering small, incremental concessions which convey flexibility and a willingness to make the deal is wiser than proposing large concessions which only whet the appetite for more and, inevitably, force you to "dig deeper" to satisfy the unreasonable expectations you've inadvertently created.

Concessions which are likely perceived as having the most value can often cost you the least, provided they address the other person's real needs. Giving an acknowledgment or praise, which might speak to his need for recognition or security, costs you nothing. So too with concessions that respond to the need for peace of mind, order and predictability, bragging rights and involvement. Smart concessions respond to fundamental human needs; they are not unthinking responses to the expression of initial wants. Statements like "I'll consider it" or "I really appreciate your help on this" are intelligent concessions.

Giving gets.

Never make a concession without getting something in return. Make your offer contingent on reciprocity: "I can do this for you, if you can do that for me." (Or, conversely, "If you can do this for me, then I can do that for you.")

Concede early on minor concerns and use this implied generosity of spirit as the foundation for seeking concessions later on major issues. Use this compelling societal propensity toward reciprocity and compromise to your advantage.

Try to conserve your price concessions for later. Remember, every negotiation has an "eleventh hour" where the horse trading is typically fast and furious. Keep sufficient concessions in reserve to ensure a satisfactory close. And, having ascertained your opposer's real needs, the longer he waits (and works) for the key concession, the greater will be his appreciation and sense of victory. That kind of intelligent giving is the fuel that drives outstanding deals.

Trust is the highest form of human motivation.

39   Specify conditions before offers.

 When it comes to building a package of reciprocal concessions that make the deal, always clarify your expectations before making final commitments.

Putting offers on the table before you've clearly specified the accompanying requirements or the anticipated concessions can unnecessarily create false impressions, give the other party an opportunity to use emotional ploys or, worse, erroneously suggest bad faith bargaining. Any of which can only produce undesirable results.

When you say "I am prepared to give you this" followed by an outline of your expectations of what the other side must now do in return for your concession, you've unnecessarily given away useful information. This is poor negotiating. The offer has already been made, admittedly with conditions, but made nonetheless. If the ensuing conditions are deemed by the other party to be unacceptable, with your position now known, the only recourse may be to reduce your otherwise legitimate expectations.

Consider the advantage that flows to you when you precede the offer by specifying your conditions: "If you are prepared to do this for me, ..." If her response to your initial condition, whether verbal or non-verbal, is positive, you can continue to add others. You can also add conditions that you do not require, thereby creating a useful concession that costs you nothing. On the other hand, just by asking, you may well succeed in securing the "add on" as well.

Specify conditions before offers.

Should the other party be unwilling or unable to concede to your initial outline of conditions, you can artfully substitute others before revealing your offer. Were your offer to have preceded the outline of accompanying conditions, their refusal would have meant a lost opportunity. Note that the creation and management of conditions and concessions is yet another function of good preparation.

This principle reinforces the critical imperative of proper, tactful and intelligent phrasing. In the giving and getting of concessions, how you say something is far more important than what you say. In addition to careful and artful phrasing designed to induce desired perceptions, the sequence of what is said can be just as important.

To maximize your impact, you must personalize both yourself and the situation.

40 Make 80/20 into 80/80.

 Regardless of the outcome, always ensure the other person leaves the negotiating table with a sense of fulfillment and satisfaction.

The happiness associated with the outcome of any negotiation is perceived, not real. How you feel about yourself, your capabilities and self-worth, will always be more important than how you feel about the deal.

A 50/50 outcome means we both got half of what was negotiated, a classic compromise. The gains were split down the middle. An 80/20 outcome means I got 80% of what was negotiated while you received the 20% that remained – in other words, a win-lose deal. An 80/80 outcome, on the other hand, is a concept that suggests there is more on the table to be negotiated and, in the end, that we can both achieve more than we initially thought possible. And why not? Since we don't need (but may want) the same thing, there's always more to be gained than we realize.

Rather than struggle to find satisfaction over the pieces of a small, finite pie, creatively we can seek to grow that pie and thereby produce bigger or perhaps more slices for both of us. This is the essence of an 80/80 outcome.

When we take stock of our gains at the conclusion of the negotiation, we must be mindful of the need to say things that will make the other person feel better about himself, and thus also his appraisal of his gains. Those words, sincerely conveyed, can enable him to rationalize and then accept a deal that might not seem as rich as yours.

Make 80/20 into 80/80.

What are some of those magical phrases you should use at the end of your negotiations? If you understand her needs, the possibilities are endless. You might, for example, compare favourably what she is paying you to what others would have had to pay. Or tell her she's getting something somebody else wanted. Compare the outcome to what she thought she would get (or to getting nothing at all). Compare it to what she originally asked for or to what you paid for it. Tell her she beat an anticipated price increase, has good taste, will be envied by others, or will be pleased with the results. Above all, tell her what a tough, but fair, negotiator she was.

Closing remarks like these are concessions that cost you nothing but reward you in many ways. Remember, in business and in life, relationships are more important than the sale. It's people who negotiate; make them feel good about themselves and they'll feel good about the deal. This is especially important in ongoing relationships because negotiators who perceive a loss invariably seek to even up the score next time around. Choose the right words at the end of your negotiation and ensure an 80/80 agreement.

People are not always what they seem.
– Gotthold Ephraim Lessing

41

Know the architecture before you build.

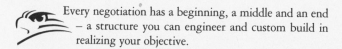 Every negotiation has a beginning, a middle and an end – a structure you can engineer and custom build in realizing your objective.

A negotiation consists of five stages. First, you must prepare. During this critical initial phase, you analyze the situation and assess the opportunity, organize your information, establish your objectives, examine leverage and determine consequences. The quality of the work done in this phase is the difference between average and great deals.

In the second stage, having done your homework, you express an opening position, create a dialogue by attending to social amenities, establish rapport, and endeavour to develop a supportive climate by reducing initial fears and concerns. Depending on the desired outcome, you mutually determine the agenda and attempt to prioritize the important items.

The third phase involves the presentation and discussion of opening positions, the gathering of information, and the identification and preliminary countering of obstacles and reservations. This stage is best described as disguise (protecting your information) and discovery (ascertaining theirs). Here you explain positions, exchange ideas, test assumptions, explore personal needs, probe for hidden information and clues to deceit, build on convergent interests, deal with resistance, and confront inappropriate and counterproductive tactics.

The fourth stage consists of the hard bargaining. Based on what you now know, you offer proposals that address concerns

Know the architecture before you build.

and resolve issues while seeking to create a package that "fits" their needs and yours. You look for innovative both-win solutions. You use contingency statements, give conditions before offers and, if necessary, find innovative ways to break an impasse.

Lastly, close and agree. This is a difficult stage as its purpose is more about optimizing gains than reaching agreement. Restate your desire for a win-win outcome. If necessary, use your last concession as an incentive for reaching agreement (or ask for something more as compensation if that decision is yours).

Summarize the agreement and get the details. Agree to what you think you already agreed upon. And always ensure through appropriate and sincere language that an 80/20 settlement is perceived as an 80/80. A good deal for you is the one that makes you happy.

While negotiating can be an emotional roller coaster, knowing the architecture and gradually building a process conducive to your objectives will make it a much smoother ride.

Well-timed silence hath more eloquence than speech.
— Martin Farquhar Tupper

42

Keep things simple and flexible.

The best negotiating strategy is one that ensures a free-flowing, spontaneous and uncomplicated dialogue.

While preparation is critical to success, that valuable time ought not be given to inordinate thought about how to convince, persuade and pressure the other party. These tactical considerations should come later, after you have developed a better appreciation and understanding of your opponent, his needs, interests, motives and aspirations.

Begin the conversation with a genuine request for information, not an accusing, judgmental and appraising demeanor. Describe what you hear to ensure the intended meaning has been received and understood. Your initial purpose is to demonstrate empathy and a willingness to experiment and innovate. In the early going, pressure tactics will only prove to be counter productive to achieving your objectives. Seek to establish a problem-solving orientation by encouraging feedback, verification and sharing.

Tactics are stress-inducing devices. Avoid unnecessary tension and conflict at the outset of the process. The typical reaction to most tactics is defensiveness. While tactics are not always easily identified, they are nonetheless either "felt" as physiological discomfort or perceived as manipulation and gamesmanship. When people feel threatened, they shut down the flow of information, become cautious, if not deceptive, and refuse to collaborate. These behaviours will not support your mission of changing their point of view.

Keep things simple and flexible.

The best strategy at the outset of your negotiation is not to have one. Be prepared but don't outthink and outmaneuvre yourself. Enter the negotiation with an open mind. Seek to gather information that will enable a better, more appropriate and artful selection of tactics for subsequent stages of the negotiation.

Create a positive first impression upon which to build your process by not appearing to have complicated or ulterior motives. People will react more favourably to your ideas and information when the situation appears straightforward and when you are viewed as being open-minded.

At the outset of negotiations, endeavour to demonstrate the attitude and behaviours of flexibility that encourage mutual sharing of information, investigation, creativity and constructive feedback. Then be prepared to reap the rewards.

*Dumb is often better than smart,
inarticulate better than articulate.*

43 Beware electronic negotiating.

 Electronic mail is a wonderful communications tool. But using it to negotiate is ill-advised. Its benefits are few and its disadvantages many.

While much is known about how people communicate in face-to-face situations, we know considerably less about electronic communications. What we do know is that it is more difficult to build trust and interpersonal chemistry. We also know that more time is required to reach agreement, that the parties participate more equally, that more information can be provided to support claims or substantiate positions, and that the incidence of insults, swearing and sarcasm is more likely.

The loss of direct eye contact, voice tone and body language depersonalizes the conversation and leads to a phenomenon known as "flaming," a no-holds-barred approach to communication. The absence of social cues can rip off the mask of civility and lay bare our innate aggressiveness. Not surprisingly, misunderstandings frequently occur.

Ideas and positions are exchanged without the benefits associated with in-person communication. Supporting gestures, mannerisms and behaviours no longer reveal important, tell-tale information. Cultural revelations and subtle assertions of gender, ethnicity and power melt away. Deprived of cues like a sign of impatience or an acid tone of voice, we may fail to discern meaningful signals.

Another potential benefit or (depending on your point of view) liability is that there is an automatic written record of all exchanges. No other form of communication is as self-documenting. Your adversary's computer now contains a file of all of your messages, which can be searched, saved, forwarded and printed as needed. Hence, your unthinking assertions and mistakes may prove costly.

It is socially easier to say "no" via e-mail than on the telephone, and easier on the telephone than face-to-face. And when e-mail is not answered promptly, we tend to wrongly assume negligence, laziness or a lack of caring about the issues.

If patience and self-control are important in electronic negotiations, good writing skills are crucial. While the computer may remove or reduce status barriers and encourage democracy, it rewards those who write well. Conversely, people who feel ill at ease expressing themselves on important issues or are uncomfortable in properly articulating and supporting their positions in writing are at a distinct disadvantage.

Use e-mail to handle the logistics and administrivia of your negotiation but strive to do the bargaining face-to-face.

You can tell whether a man is clever by his answers.
You can tell whether a man is wise by his questions.
– Mahfouz Naguib

44 The telephone isn't the answer either.

 Telephone negotiations are quick and extremely risky. If you have no alternative, understand how to use it and what the liabilities are.

Despite the risks, telephone negotiations are an inevitable part of daily business life. The obvious disadvantage is that access to important non-verbal cues is denied. We must rely instead on tone of voice which is more easily feigned. Moreover, there is less opportunity for sustained interpersonal involvement and, thus, less chance to ascertain compelling needs. And the efficiency of the telephone prevents us from investing time in building the process.

If you must negotiate on the telephone, always be the caller. The one who answers is, by definition, usually unprepared and more likely to be "taken by surprise." In answering the phone, you have been denied the most important stage of the negotiating process – preparation. Your thoughts are elsewhere as is the file you may need to consult.

If you are called, find a plausible excuse to call back. In some extreme situations, that may even require you to literally hang up on yourself. (Don't worry, because this action is not a common business practice, the caller's perception will be that you got cut off.) Since she cannot see your immediate environment, "there's someone in my office right now – I'll call you back" should be a sufficient and acceptable response.

In preparing to make (or return) the call, remind yourself of the principles of good preparation. Think through the result you

The telephone isn't the answer either.

want to achieve and develop an appropriate strategy. Prepare a check-list or a script beforehand which contains the points you want to cover, the concessions you're willing to make, and the objectives you want to achieve. Since your discussion outline can't be seen by the other party, you can place it on your desk in front of you during the call.

When negotiating by telephone across time zones, it is wise not to call near the end of your alter negotiator's business day. However, with some Asian and mid-Eastern cultures, you should anticipate that that's precisely when you are likely to be called. (An understanding of cultural differences is critical if your negotiations are to be conducted by telephone or electronically.)

If the negotiation is of major significance, dry run your script with a colleague or spouse, someone who can give you helpful feedback on your style. Close the door to avoid distractions. Discipline yourself to listen and take notes for review later. If you are placed in an awkward position, hear a difficult demand, or need to build some pressure, say nothing. On the telephone, a "pregnant pause" is at its most powerful

Trying to "teach someone a lesson" never works.
— Men's Health

45 Persistence can pay huge rewards.

 Persistence, dogged determination and patience are to power and negotiating leverage what carbon is to steel.

A negotiation is fundamentally an investment of time and effort. The more time and effort you invest, the greater is the likelihood of being justly rewarded. When people invest, they do so in search of a return of some kind. When they invest smartly – by doing the right things at the right time – they are rarely disappointed. The same principle applies to increasing your winning percentage at the bargaining table.

Persistence is the one form of power we can all possess. We may not have sufficient money, we may be limited in our options and we may lack status but we can surely be more patient, if not tenacious, in the pursuit of our objectives.

Persistence is the inevitable bi-product of understanding the need for process. It's an appreciation that the structure of a negotiation takes time to build, especially in the presence of an unwilling or uncooperative adversary. It's an understanding that time changes everything and that tactics require appropriate timing to be effective. And it's being mindful of the need for repetition, which leads to learning (and the eventual acceptance of your point of view).

Others have spoken eloquently about the value of persistence. Dr. Samuel Jackson said that "Great works are performed not by strength but by perseverance." While strength is obviously power, so too is persistence.

Persistence can pay huge rewards.

The American President, Calvin Coolidge, went further: "Nothing in the world can take the place of persistence. Talent will not; nothing is more common than the unsuccessful man with talent. Genius will not; unrewarded genius is almost a proverb. Education will not; the world is full of educated derelicts. Persistence and determination alone are omnipotent. The slogan 'press on' has solved and always will solve the problems of the human race."

Whenever your negotiations seem difficult or complex, or when you doubt your power, just "hang in there" a little longer. By refusing to interrupt their words or thoughts, by resisting the temptation to interject your own reservations, by not filling the vacuum of silence, and by understanding that time does indeed change everything, you will become a better negotiator. Persistence is always rewarded.

The words you choose to say something
are just as important as the decision to speak.

46   Read their signals.

 Intentionally or not, negotiators emit meaningful signals. Know how to identify, interpret and reciprocate these telltale cues to confirm or deny pertinent information.

Signals can be both verbal and non-verbal. They are often used to mask or feign the importance of the information being provided. Signals can also be clues to deceit. Minimally, once revealed and understood, they are opportunities to avoid being put at a competitive disadvantage.

Here is an example. Along with price and other considerations in your negotiation, you are discussing the delivery of an item. In response to your request for a commitment (since delivery is important to you), you hear: "Off the top of my head, Sue, I can have it to you by Friday." If you listened to the specific words spoken, the commitment you seek has been undermined by the phrase that precedes it.

"Off the top of my head" is a verbal signal worthy of your attention and further exploration. It suggests the delivery date may be at risk. It's certainly not firm and that's precisely what you need to know before you can respond with a complementary or further concession. Having identified the signal, you need to confirm the commitment by asking: "Is there any reason why it might not be there on Friday?" Now, if there is a problem with the date, you will likely be told.

To detect signals that might potentially reveal critical information, listen to the exact words spoken and tactfully question any that are imprecise, inconsistent or inaccurate. There is a big

Read their signals.

difference between claims like "difficult" *vs.* "impossible" or "can't" *vs.* "won't." These are signals, usually unintentional, worth clarifying and exploring further.

Signals are also non-verbal. Rather than saying "off the top of my head," your alter negotiator tentatively rubs the bridge of his nose at the precise moment he says "It'll be there on Friday." This particular gesture has a number of possible meanings. It might suggest doubt, reservation or, in the extreme, denial. All of which are contrary to what has been said.

Never expose a signal that's been given; it's yours to decipher. But do act on your instinct that there may be a problem that needs to be aired, identified and confirmed. Some signals should be filed away for later. "Maybe" might suggest a softness in the position and that should be discussed when more concrete proposals and concessions are made.

Every negotiator sends signals, usually unwittingly. Read them and use them to your advantage. And be mindful of your own signals – what might they be telling the other side?

Never negotiate without options.

47 Objections are masked opportunities.

 View an objection to your proposal as an expression of genuine interest in the proposition and an indication of a need to better understand its benefits and relevance.

Your point of view determines your behaviour. If you choose to see objections as indicators of doubt, reservation or resistance, they become precisely that. Alternatively, if you see them as a plea for information, you will begin to ask questions, search for common ground, and propose creative options that might satisfy their needs and your objectives.

In a negotiation, objections are neither interruptions nor rejections but an integral part of the process. Without objections there is no negotiation. So the first time you hear an objection, ignore it. In the absence of support or further resistance, most objections evaporate. The purpose was simply to state them, not debate them.

When a buyer says, "Your price is too high," don't defend your position. Rather, say "I understand" or "Uh huh." Don't assume people are seeking agreement with their concerns; they may simply want an acknowledgment of their point of view. If the objection is repeated, however, it merits a reply.

Diffuse the intensity of the reservation by using the following sequence of responses. First, pace the discussion, ask questions and gather information. Use good reflection skills and attempt to discover the reason for the objection. Once you better understand the concern, creatively redefine or "reframe" the meaning or the consequences of the reservation: "While I hear you saying

Objections are masked opportunities.

you can't afford it right now, can you really afford to lose this opportunity?" Next propose an alternative (a "What if ...?" suggestion) that comes closer to satisfying the objection: "What if we were to lower the up-front payment and reduce or eliminate the add-ons that might not be required until later?"

If, after going through this process, you realize the objection is valid, simply agree with it. Don't entrench or energize the opposition. Move on. As you're discovering, there are many other points of leverage in a negotiation.

Objections are useful in discovering hidden needs. They can tell us what's important to the other party. If you anticipate an objection (yet another reason for sound preparation), it's wise to try to diffuse or pre-empt it in advance. Alternatively, change the topic and see if it evaporates on its own.

When all else fails, follow the salesman's dictum: If they object to the price, talk about the quality. If they object to quality, talk about service. If they object to service, talk about terms. If they object to terms, then talk about price. Just keep them talking.

Power is not only what you have
but what the enemy thinks you have.
– Saul Alinsky

48 Be wary of assumptions.

 Untested assumptions stand in the way of creative problem solving and contribute to unnecessary conflict. Always challenge assumptions, yours as well as theirs.

It is human nature to make assumptions. We like to think we don't make too many assumptions but, unfortunately, that is just not the case. We act on the information we think we know or, worse, think we should know. In tests designed to measure the extent of this human propensity, subjects are invariably startled by the number of assumptions made on the basis of minimal and even uncomplicated messages.

When information is consciously concealed or withheld, as typically occurs in a negotiation, we are compelled to make even more assumptions. Since conflict distorts communication and impairs listening, imagine how many assumptions are made in the stressful environment of the bargaining arena, when emotions are aroused and information is purposefully disguised?

Assumptions are usually self-fulfilling. Research demonstrates that when people assume a task to be difficult or complex, it often becomes difficult and complex. If you assume the other person will ridicule your opening offer, you will probably modify it on your own in order to make it more acceptable, *i.e.*, what you believe would be a more acceptable position.

Making assumptions is a way of rationalizing unintentional or poor performance. If you think you have all the information you require to make a good decision, you will stop asking

Be wary of assumptions.

pertinent, probing questions. These and other poor decisions are based on false perceptions, erroneous assumptions and stereotypical thinking that, if untested, will be counterproductive to achieving your objectives.

We all make assumptions. To negotiate effectively, you must acknowledge and confront that reality, both in your planning and in your performance at the negotiating table. You must endeavour to become more conscious of the assumptions you are making about the other person, the situation at hand and the issues in dispute.

There is an antidote to making too many false assumptions. The cure lies in asking a lot of artful, discerning, intelligent questions. When it doubt, don't assume – ask, explore, test and challenge.

Leave a good name in case you return.
– Kenyan folk saying

49

How you say it is important.

 Optimal negotiators choose their words carefully. They know that how something is said is more important than what is said.

In setting a climate conducive to realizing your objectives, customize your words to fit the other person's self-image and frame of reference. Seek to be understood and ignore the ego temptation to impress, entertain or, worse, bully.

Call it verbal gymnastics, semantics or whatever you like, but an occasional euphemism will get your point across while disarming a hostile adversary. Thoughtful phrasing will induce different perceptions and thus different, perhaps desired, answers. If a courtroom witness is asked to estimate the speed of a vehicle that "ran" into another, the answer will likely be different from that given when the same question contains the verb "smashed" (into the other car). Repetitive emphasis serves the same purpose. Contrast the persuasiveness of "Did you see the child?" with "You did see the child, didn't you?" Never doubt the importance of choosing your words wisely to achieve your objectives.

To convince people, deliver your message in a way that appeals to their needs, not yours. Be mindful that it's much easier to make a decision against something rather than for something. Reflect on the fact that people understand what they experience more so than what they hear (and they remember about 10% of what is heard as contrasted with 90% of what they do). Let them experience the reasons for your conclusions by making it real and therefore meaningful for them.

How you say it is important.

Persuasion is more likely to occur when you begin by agreeing with people and focusing on convergent interests. This initial agreement helps to build trust. "I can understand why you would say (or feel) that" is a good way to turn a resistant state of mind into one that is more receptive. Never challenge the other person's values. Placing her on the defensive will not succeed in convincing her. You want information, not resistance and entrenchment.

When asking sensitive questions, preface them with an appropriate non-threatening rationale. She will respond according to her internal cost-benefit analysis, not yours. Outline the benefits and then move her slowly, incrementally toward your desired position. Help her transition to your point of view by introducing new and credible information.

Reinforce co-operative behaviour with positive social bonding responses (like a smile, wink or nod) and positive psychological strokes and validation (*e.g.*, "It sounds like you've given this a lot of thought"). The goal in influencing behaviour and persuading others is always progress, not perfection.

*Power is never constant. Even the passage of time
will cause your leverage to change.*

50 The best concessions may cost nothing.

Never give away more than is necessary. It serves no purpose other than to whet your alter negotiator's appetite for even more and thereby inadvertently contribute to his disappointment.

Successful negotiating is satisfying needs, not accommodating wants. Consider, for example, an employment interview. While the focus is primarily on resolving compensation issues, there is much to be gained by knowing deeper needs and desires. Is the job candidate motivated by career development opportunities, by title or by the expectations of family members? Perhaps relocation is an issue; in which case, recommending a reliable carrier for the home furnishings may be seen as an important concession – because, unknown to you, among the family's prized possessions is an heirloom that has been passed down over generations. Having this cherished item arrive safely is a "priceless" consideration. And yet another concession that costs you nothing.

The same thinking might apply to the spouse who is affected by the relocation. Giving him a job as well is poor negotiating. Recommending solid contacts in the community that might enable him to land a position is smart bargaining. A daughter who aspires to attend university shouldn't automatically receive the company scholarship; rather, pending an agreement between the parties, she would be given the "opportunity" to apply. Providing references that will help ease the family into this new community enable a peace of mind that cannot be underestimated. Too frequently, we give away more than is required and thereby limit our own options.

The best concessions may cost nothing.

In most organizations, bosses are protected by "company policy" that effectively limits the scope of negotiating. While, in part, that is the purpose of such policies, they should not prohibit you from testing and challenging same when they are used as an attempt to constrain bargaining.

From the boss's perspective, consider the negotiating leverage that ensues from making someone an "exception to the rule" (regardless of the degree of variation from what the policy dictates). By making this slight accommodation, something that likely costs very little, you have acknowledged that the person before you is different. And that perception on the other side of the table has value beyond mere numbers. After all, what price can you place on bragging rights and on feeling special?

Statements that acknowledge people's basic needs are valued concessions. "Thanks, I appreciate that" is a concession. So too is an empathic response like "I understand how you feel about this." "Let me see what I can do for you" suggests a willingness to accommodate the other person's problems. Take the time to look beyond the numbers to respond to needs, interests, feelings and aspirations and you will discover concessions that cost little but go a long way towards making great deals.

Jaw-jaw is better than war-war.
— Harold Macmillan

51   Make the pressure explicit.

 The greatest fear is fear of the unknown. Optimal negotiators eliminate, or at least reduce, the pressure they
might feel by making their fears and concerns explicit.

Consider the pressure implied in a threat such as, "If we don't
do it my way, I'll quit!" The threat clearly articulates the consequences of the ultimatum. Should you disagree with "his
way," you know he'll leave. You are now able to assess the
merits or costs of his departure in the context of the advantages
and disadvantages of conceding to his demand. You have the
information needed to make a rational choice.

Conversely, if the threat were to suggest an unknown outcome
(such as, "If we don't do it my way, my options are limited"),
you would surely feel greater pressure. You don't know what
his options are. Might he quit? Perhaps. But he didn't say he
would. Might he mean lurking in the shadows some night with
a baseball bat ready to cause you harm? Who really knows?
The pressure is squarely upon you to figure out the consequences
of his vague "limited options."

Before the negotiation, take the time to identify and reflect on
your pressure points. Then consider what hers might be. Is
your pressure a time constraint, limited resources, insufficient
information, the unrealistic expectations of your superiors, or
something else?

We enter negotiations surrounded by the pressure of our own
expectations, perceptions and concerns. Take a moment to
make a list of those pressures. Then think of creative ways you

Make the pressure explicit.

might disguise them. Alternatively, it may be strategically advantageous to reveal some of them in an artful manner. The more you think about them, and the options for dealing with them, the less stressful they will become.

Now make a list of her pressures. Admittedly, you may not know what they are so assume what they might be or, alternatively, mirror your own list. Might she not have to deal with the same challenges and constraints as you?

Now consider ways to discover or expose them, perhaps with probing and presumptive questions like "I guess your boss has big expectations of you on this deal." Regardless of her answer, the body language and tonality of the response will indicate whether you've uncovered a pressure point that might be to your subsequent advantage.

Don't ignore pressure points. Bring them to the surface where you can deal with them in a creative, intelligent and rational way. Assumptions and unknown fears cause pressure – the more explicit they are, the less pressure you feel.

You can get much further with a kind word and a gun than you can with a kind word alone.
– Al Capone

52 Agendas are assets worth having.

Just as agendas are boilerplate in sophisticated negotiating arenas, like collective bargaining and international diplomacy, they can be equally useful in enhancing interpersonal bargaining.

Agendas do many things. An agenda provides a structure for conflict resolution. Despite the emotional intensity at the outset of the negotiation, the parties can readily see that their needs and issues will be addressed at some point during the discussion. Agendas are information gathering devices – they enable you to see the other's concerns and to prepare accordingly. Those who might be unwilling to give information early in the negotiating process can be compelled to do so via an agenda. And agendas make "hidden agendas" transparent.

Agendas should be used strategically. He who controls the agenda has power. When both parties understand that important premise, they invariably establish ground rules for agenda setting. In other words, agenda determination can itself become a critical part of the negotiation.

Agendas are good meeting management tools: they not only facilitate preparation, they enable the issues to be prioritized, keep negotiations focussed and on track, and assist in the recording of what was discussed.

Agendas can also be used tactically. Should you, for example, position the most contentious issue at the start or at the end of the agenda? It depends on your objectives: you may want to deal with lesser items first to create a sense of momentum.

Agendas are assets worth having.

Alternatively, the smaller issues may be useful bargaining chips for sweetening the deal at the end. You might add items to an agenda so as to afford more win-win trade-offs or you can limit the negotiation by removing irrelevant topics.

Agendas enable you to quickly see and assess potential packages and trade-offs or, by using it as an information-giving device, to alter expectations. Or you can overload an agenda and thereby ensure a time-out and follow-up meeting.

Clearly, agendas are powerful tools that serve useful purposes in negotiating, whether the focus be on the resolution of business or even personal issues. If you haven't used an agenda in negotiating with a teenager or spouse, try it. You'll discover its value as a vehicle for ascertaining needed information that can enable both-win solutions. Do what the pros do – use agendas both strategically and tactically to enhance outcomes.

Plan your work and work your plan.
– Peter Drucker

53   The first offer is not the final offer.

Optimal negotiators know there is a difference between what people say they want and what they really want. Give yourself the time needed to discover that difference.

The opening marks the beginning of a long and sometimes arduous process. Regardless of your adversary's initial position, never overreact. Should you think your alter negotiator has opened too high, some humour in your rebuttal might be appropriate. Say something like, "You're just kidding, right?" or "I'd probably get fired if I agreed to that price."

Avoid ridicule, put-downs or personal abuse, especially in front of others. Reject a high (or low) starting position without rejecting the person who made it. Remind yourself that she either perceives it to be right for this phase of bargaining or it is little more than a tactic designed to lower your own expectations.

Take your time. Even if he says his price is firm, recognize that it is only his starting position. Your actions and words should be geared toward reducing his aspirations and increasing his anxiety. You want to create the impression that, by continuing to negotiate, a satisfactory agreement for both parties will be found. So, at the outset, avoid a hard "no" (say "maybe" and "perhaps" instead). Remember, the opening position and its presentation is likely important to him on a personal level. He has prepared for this and his reputation or feeling of self-worth is at stake.

Should you feel like reacting emotionally, take a time-out to test your initial assumptions. That too can send a powerful

The first offer is not the final offer.

message without committing yourself to a response. Ask her for more information, *e.g.*, get a price breakdown and analyze it – you'll likely find negotiating ammunition in the breakdown that will require her to defend the opening (and thus provide further grist for a better rebuttal).

Hear out the opening in its entirety. By interjecting too early, you might miss a soft area or signal worth probing later. Be patient, take notes, ask further questions but do not be critical during this opening phase. Model the behaviour you expect of your alter negotiator.

When you've decided on an appropriate response, insist that she listen to your full rebuttal ... just as you listened attentively to her opening position. At the start, you're not only gathering valuable information, you're demonstrating how you want the negotiation to proceed. This role modeling of appropriate behaviour will pay dividends later. Your response should send a clear message that you take the opening number to be no more than the beginning of a *quid pro quo* process.

The harder the conflict, the more glorious the triumph.
– Thomas Paine

54 A change can break an impasse.

 Like objections, impasse is simply part of the negotiating process. The antidote is to change something.

Most deadlocks in business negotiations involve discussions of money. To break the impasse, propose a change in either the terms or medium of exchange. A larger deposit, a shorter payment period, or an otherwise different approach to cash flow can work wonders even though the total amount of money remains the same. A smaller percentage of a larger amount or a larger percentage of a smaller but more predictable base may also get things back on track. Change the specifications of the task while leaving the price constant. Alternatively, add options of a real or apparent nature. The offer of options that are unlikely to be taken may be sufficient to move an otherwise questionable deal forward.

Another approach to breaking deadlock, if appropriate, is to change the negotiators. In a team bargaining scenario, change the gender of the chief spokesperson or replace a team member whose behaviour is perceived to be counterproductive to advancing the process. Likewise, you could call in a mediator or facilitator or arrange a summit meeting or "hot-line" call to an absent key decision maker. Align the personalities – get engineers involved with engineers, older people with older people, bosses with bosses. Set up a joint study committee or find a different structure for dealing with the contentious issues.

Change the shape of risk or uncertainty. Postpone difficult issues for renegotiation at a later time when more information is known or just to give the parties time to think or restore their

A change can break an impasse.

composure. A willingness to share unknown losses or gains that cannot be accurately forecast may reduce perceived risk. Likewise, future satisfaction or reassurance might be heightened by recommending grievance procedures, conflict resolution protocols, guarantees or warranties.

The negotiating process and the climate itself can be altered. Disclosure of relevant information or unanticipated minor concessions can move the negotiation forward. Change the bargaining emphasis from a competitive mode to one of collaboration and co-operative problem solving. Break the tension – tell a funny story.

And so it goes. Impasse can be broken just by doing something differently. All it takes is an assessment of the consequences of continued deadlock, creativity and a willingness to be flexible.

The fellow that agrees with everything you say is either a fool or he is getting ready to skin you. – Ken Hubbard

55   Deadlock is not a dirty word.

While an impasse can be broken, creating one can serve a useful purpose. If you always make the deal, your negotiating style becomes predictable, thereby ensuring the other party always gets the last concession.

A deadlock enhances the perception of risk. The thought that all the time and effort invested thus far may be for naught can be stressful. If you are not willing to occasionally walk away from the table, or feign the intention of doing so, your persuasiveness over time will be undermined. If they know you will always make the deal, the threat of impasse as your only alternative is compromised or transparent.

Becoming an optimal negotiator requires you to become more comfortable, confident and competent with principles such as this. Unless and until you try to do something different, you will feel awkward and unsure just contemplating that action. You will naturally wonder whether the tactic will work or fail. You will then logically assume it will be at some cost or discomfort to yourself. It doesn't take much to talk yourself out of good tactics.

The same applies to deliberately creating an impasse for a purpose. Simply by doing it, you will discover your negotiation has not necessarily come to an end. But your predictability as a negotiator certainly has. Remember as well that there are a multitude of creative ways to resume the discussion.

Deadlock should be used as a tactic to underscore the seriousness of your position or, when acting as a limited agent for someone

Deadlock is not a dirty word.

else, to convey an important message to a decision maker or to your constituents.

Union-management bargaining is frequently protracted by design, in part to ensure that the rank-and-file membership clearly understands how difficult the negotiations are and thus to confirm their wisdom in electing a group of tough negotiators to represent their best interests. It can also ensure that the eventual recommendation for settlement will be taken more seriously by the members.

Credibility notwithstanding, some negotiators will often, almost characteristically, use impasse as a bargaining tactic. This too is unwise. Given the downside risk, such predictability is a definite liability. That being said, there are times when it is entirely appropriate to create a deadlock. This should happen whenever you are asked to compromise your principles.

Social bonding is impossible in the absence of humour.

56   Know when to close.

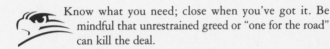 Know what you need; close when you've got it. Be mindful that unrestrained greed or "one for the road" can kill the deal.

Many people know how to negotiate but don't have a clue about when to make the deal. Closing, or getting all that you can without compromising your objectives, is a critically important but difficult part of the negotiating process. Know where you're going and prepare for your close along the way. Endeavour to assume the end position in what you say and do.

Your bargaining posture – the magnitude and frequency of your concessions – must not only reinforce the impact and credibility of your opening position but also give you sufficient latitude to close a favourable deal. Accordingly, as you get closer to your desired end point, your concessions must become fewer, smaller and harder to obtain.

Make closing both pleasant and positive for the other person. It should be seen as a natural, inevitable consequence of the direction the negotiation has taken to that point. Don't put too much pressure on him. Nudge, don't shove. Hesitations are not refusals. Sustain your enthusiasm for making a deal. Don't make statements that might leave guilt feelings, such as suggesting or implying how much better he might have done. That is allowing your ego to get in the way of your objective.

Close by getting agreement first on the principle or issue, then on the price. Deal with their objections openly and honestly.

Know when to close.

Agree with their concerns if you cannot negate them. Empathize, don't object. Provide helpful information, then ask questions that imply a close, such as "Would you like that in red or blue?" Learn to stop talking when the close is imminent. Let the momentum of the negotiation and the mutual desire to achieve something in return for the time and effort invested carry you forward.

If you are asking for the deal to be made, always keep at least one concession back. If necessary, you can trade it as an inducement for the agreement. Conversely, if the agreement is yours to make, then ask for a concession as compensation.

Once you have an agreement, go over the deal one more time. Agree to what you have already agreed to ensure there are no "fuzzies." Remember, people do forget – sometimes for tactical reasons, sometimes for convenience and sometimes because their memories are genuinely impaired. Restate and confirm the agreement. Should you feel the need to create an 80/80 outcome, a further concession might be given after the agreement is reached.

The purpose of a negotiation is to negotiate for a purpose.

57   Close with magic.

 People agree for one of two reasons: either to gain a benefit or to avoid a loss. The best closing statements always stress the benefits to the buyer.

Phrasing is always critical to your negotiating success but it is especially important in framing the closing position. Use terms that appear advantageous to the other party while delivering on your own objectives. A good closing proposition might be phrased as follows: "If you thought you could actually get (benefit 1), (benefit 2) and (benefit 3) by accepting this deal, would you do so?"

Alternatively, you could say, "If you felt you could actually reach and inform the prospect you want to reach, and thus get more business by using the resources of our agency, would you do so?" When overcoming objections, a good closing line might be something like this: "If I could resolve those problems (or concerns) to your satisfaction, would you feel better about accepting my proposal?"

A sound closing strategy is one that removes the pressure on the buyer while ensuring you get the credit for doing so. Elicit his help in identifying and addressing the real concerns. For example, you might say: "I'm not here to pressure you into making a bad decision. I'm here to give you the information you will need to make a good decision. How can I do that to your satisfaction?"

Rather than openly confronting and possibly energizing an obstacle raised during the closing, endeavour to dilute or

Close with magic.

reframe it. Any perceived resistance to an objection will only provide further ammunition to oppose your closing proposition.

The best way to dilute an objection or reservation at closing is to try to understand it better. The effort perceived in doing so will be appreciated by your alter negotiator. Ask a question, such as: "Is that your only reason?" This sort of question usually prompts a follow-up (but weaker) argument which is a natural defensive response. A variation on this question aimed at defusing objections is: "So those are your only reasons? You don't have any more?" This helps to ensure there are no further hidden points of resistance.

The art of closing with magic lies in choosing the right words. A good deal is the one that makes both parties happy. How you choose to say it – by alleviating concerns and demonstrating empathy and understanding – will contribute substantially to that perceived level of happiness.

Most people never listen.
– Ernest Hemingway

58 Critically assess your performance.

 After every important negotiation, take the time and effort to critically evaluate your performance and the reasons why you succeeded or failed.

Most negotiators tend to rationalize their results, aggrandizing good deals while "explaining away" the bad ones. Optimal negotiators endeavour to learn from each and every experience. They take the opportunity to experiment with and to practice, refine and adapt the guiding principles. The advice and insights to be found in these pages are little more than just good words until you put them to the test of your own experience and then assess the results. Comfort and confidence come with the execution of the counsel. The proof is in the performance. While the theory might help you understand, the reality of benefitting from it is a function of application and evaluation.

When I instruct the participants in my courses on negotiating principles, their understanding and subsequent learning are predicated largely on a comparative, clinical self-assessment of their performance in simulated negotiating exercises. This is when we take the time to evaluate the students' personal negotiating experiences and tactics to ascertain whether they are indeed trying to do things differently and, if so, with what results. This period of reflection is always informative.

The "Insanity Principle" stipulates that we can't produce different results by continuing to do the same thing. So, whenever you experiment with new negotiating approaches, techniques and principles, you need to review and measure the results by answering a series of questions not unlike these:

Critically assess your performance.

- Aside from the issues being negotiated, what was the biggest personal obstacle to reaching an agreement?
- To what degree were you satisfied (or dissatisfied) with your negotiation? Why do you feel this way?
- Which of your tactics was especially helpful in moving the negotiation toward a satisfactory conclusion?
- What actions or behaviours on your part tended to prevent or impair the outcome you sought?
- When did you have your strongest feelings? What emotions were you experiencing? How did you address them?
- Apart from your emotions, what pressures were you feeling and why? How might you deal with them in the future?
- How did your alter negotiator's style affect yours? Why?
- What have you learned? What would you do differently the next time?

Like all great performers, optimal negotiators are conscientious and continuous learners. Honest answers to tough questions like these will make you one too.

Good questions outrank easy answers.
— Paul A. Samuelson

59

Practice when it doesn't count.

 The adage "practice makes perfect" applies to negotiators. Yet few take the time to practice, preferring instead to negotiate only when it must be done.

The notion that you might forego a rerun of your favourite television program for the opportunity to visit a local car dealership or appliance store to practice and refine your retail bargaining skills may strike you as ludicrous. However, using your precious recreational time to hone your bargaining skills will ensure a measurable, perhaps even significant return on that investment, especially when it comes time to negotiate "for real" – as inevitably it will.

When you practice, there is no pressure. You can test tactics for appropriate phrasing and effect without the worry of failure or the stress that invariably accompanies situations in which you feel you "must buy" the item being negotiated. You can experiment with deadlock or "walking away" and you can better understand the needs of limited agents and their superiors (the real decision makers).

With practice, you will develop a higher comfort zone around the use of body language to make your point. And, without the normal tension that accompanies negotiating for real, you will become more adept at detecting the meaning and capturing the significance of your alter negotiator's non-verbal gestures and clues to deceit. These are among the things we fail to consider when the interaction is more purposeful.

Practice when it doesn't count.

Prepare for difficult or complex negotiations by using role plays. Encourage your practice partner to ask the tough questions you hope will never be asked (but invariably are).

Preparing good answers to tough questions isn't enough, however. Since how you say something is more important that what you say, practice phrasing your answers so they not only disguise but are viewed as credible. This skill and comfort level only comes with good planning and repetition. The objective is to ensure proper voice tone, spontaneity and supporting body language are consistent with the message you intend to deliver.

Just as great athletes practice to develop muscle memory and great actors rehearse to ensure they don't flub their lines on stage, you too can perfect the subtleties and nuances that come with being an optimal negotiator. Practice enables you to obtain confidence and competence in the execution of new skills. With that foundation, eventually comes mastery.

When you know all the answers,
you haven't asked all the questions.

60

Avoid a dialogue of the deaf.

Negotiation is fundamentally an act of communication. The better the communication, the richer the outcome. That happens when *both* negotiators understand what is being communicated.

Unfortunately, too many negotiators play a game of semantic ping-pong in which words, rather than meanings, are exchanged. Optimal negotiators realize that meaning is in the receiver, not in the sender. It matters not what we say to people; what counts is what they hear. And never assume people hear what you intend to tell them.

For a variety of reasons, ranging from one's psychological state of mind to noise and visual distractions, people hear only what they want to hear and what their circumstances and social conditioning have prepared them to hear. Reflecting on that basic premise will make you a better negotiator and encourage you to communicate within the other's frame of reference. If the objective is to make your point and have it accepted, that's the only frame that counts.

Too often, the sender of a message operates on the premise that what she has to say includes all that is worth saying. She forgets that effective communication is a shared experience. When miscommunication occurs, she assumes it to be a result of the listener's disagreement with her clearly articulated views. Yet, more often than not, disagreement arises from different perceptions of the same situation. So, taking the time to understand how the other person "filters" your words is crucial to successfully delivering your message.

Avoid a dialogue of the deaf.

The sender presumes she is communicating whenever she speaks. In truth, she communicates only when the receiver accepts, understands, and is influenced by her words. She fancies that communication is simply a matter of saying the right thing at the right time in the right way. This is important but not paramount. We also communicate via vocal intonation and inflection as well as facial expression and body language, which research tells us actually account for most of the meaning in our messages.

Never assume that you have a person's undivided attention. What we might perceive to be attention giving is often little more than selective inattention.

People listen to what they find real and meaningful for them. To avoid a dialogue of the deaf, make your message pertinent and intelligible to the other person's world. Communication should be a dialogue within a framework of mutual interests and needs, not a process of unilateral bludgeoning.

Losing is nothing but a series of small compromises.

61 Craft a message that appeals.

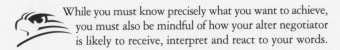 While you must know precisely what you want to achieve, you must also be mindful of how your alter negotiator is likely to receive, interpret and react to your words.

Communication is a human transaction. People influence people. Before you begin communicating, take a moment to reflect on how your words and phrasing might stir his interest or arouse her enthusiasm. Think about, or try to discover, what leaves him cold and indifferent, what annoys him or makes him touchy, and what his hot buttons might be. Be sensitive to her contrary but nonetheless legitimate objectives and learn to communicate value according to her definition of what is valuable. Remember, in virtually every negotiation, the other person has but one question in mind: "What's in it for me?"

In face-to-face communication, manner is more important than meaning. If she does not like your manner, she probably will not buy your meaning. Since negotiation is a dialogue, allow ample time for the other person to get her "oar in the water." Be sensitive to the impact of silence; it can speak volumes and is hard to refute.

It is difficult to relate to someone who knows everything. Try to create a climate of acceptance for what you say even though she may not want to hear it. Be aware of her biases. Be equally sensitive to your own preferences and aversions. Understand that the language of feelings is more compelling than the language of the intellect.

Craft a message that appeals.

To become a persuasive communicator, consider this advice:
- It is more effective to present both sides of an issue – people listen better when you acknowledge their position.
- Whenever you outline pros and cons, present your strongest position last – don't weaken it with afterthoughts.
- Wants should be explicitly stated, not left for the other person to assume or deduce.
- A message that arouses a need, then provides a supporting reason, will be remembered best.
- People can disagree with your number but not the reason behind it.
- Positions viewed as threatening will likely be rejected.
- People will act on their ideas before they act on yours.
- People push back on requested opinion change so ask for more than you expect.
- Acceptance is improved when the message is repeated and when stress is placed on similarities of interests.
- Agreement is more likely when the desirability of reaching agreement is made explicit.
- People who place others on the defensive rarely succeed in convincing them.

An ounce of appearance is worth a pound of substance.

62 Be a non-directional listener.

Optimal negotiators are good listeners. This skill, and the patience that accompanies it, enables them to make sound decisions based on the information, opinions and insights others provide.

An attentive listener not only stimulates better speaking, she learns to distinguish fact from opinion, evaluate inferences and reasoning, detect prejudices and assumptions, and restructure vague proposals into clearer meaning. If information is power, listening is the method of accruing it.

Non-directional listening occurs when you refuse to render an opinion on what has been said. It is non-judgmental listening. This behaviour motivates the speaker to continue talking and, in the process, provides more and better information. It produces a calming effect on the speaker and is helpful in generating a climate conducive to mutual problem solving.

To be a non-directional listener, you must take the time to listen. Though you may think that listening to something you don't want to hear is a waste of time, it seldom is – especially in a negotiation where the objective is to get behind the words to ascertain the real needs, issues and concerns. If, by listening, you can help him clear his mind and prompt deeper understanding, it will not only help improve the quality of the information provided but also make him a more attentive listener when its your turn to speak.

Employ verbal reactions that don't imply judgement – a series of supportive grunts or words such as: "Hmm," "Oh," or "I see." If the talker pauses momentarily, remain silent or nod your head to indicate continuing interest and understanding, thus encouraging her to resume speaking. Never probe for additional facts. In a negotiation, a willingness to listen is better than a curious inquisitiveness designed to obtain information. Be attentive.

If a tirade is launched, the best response is to let it flow uninterrupted until it's been exhausted. Since "all of you" is communicating (words, voice tone and non-verbal gestures), seek to understand what is being said. Validate feelings – the more she feels the information is important, the more likely she will continue to provide it.

Refrain from evaluating or giving advice, even if asked to do so. Passing judgement on what is being said or, worse, correcting same will only produce defensiveness, effectively shutting down communications. Never underestimate the talker's ability to solve his own problems or come up with a creative alternative. When the other person is given the opportunity to speak his mind, you may be amazed by some of the suggestions or ideas that might likewise address your needs.

Knowledge is power.
– Francis Bacon

63   Ask the right questions.

Optimal negotiators ask questions skillfully and with purpose. The answers keep the dialogue moving forward, provide guidance on what to say next and give assurance that the objective is achievable.

In formulating your questions, apply the following rules. Good questions neither offend nor convey status or authority. They are characterized by civility and respect and phrased in a tentative and understanding way to create a climate of co-operation and to motivate your alter negotiator to give candid replies.

Good questions are those phrased to ascertain needed information for the purpose of reaching agreement, not those that invade the other's privacy. They do not make one feel uncomfortable, nor do they cause anxiety. They are helpful to both parties and not worded as blatant attempts at manipulation.

Artful questions are not stated in such a manner that they appear tricky, emotionally loaded, devious, embarrassing, double-barreled or petty. They should build on each other, be appropriate to the situation and designed to achieve a specific objective rather than just elicit an answer.

Whenever feasible, it is advisable to offer a premise that explains the reason for asking a question and to avoid asking intrusive questions that place others on the defensive (*e.g.* questions, such as "What's your excuse?"). A non-forcing question, like "How do you feel about this issue?" permits fuller, more meaningful disclosure and encourages further discussion. As always, tone of voice and appropriate phrasing are important to ensure

Ask the right questions.

clarity of your intention and to avoid false inferences.

Consider also the timing of your questions. The objective should be to guide the other negotiator in deciding what he should say next. The inopportune timing of a question, such as "Do you like this plan?", may well freeze your opponent into an immovable position.

Ask open-ended, specific yet simple questions that enable you to build your information base gradually and with intent. ("How do you feel about this plan?" will evoke far more useful information than the question previously noted.) Good questions come from good planning.

Your questions should be designed with the primary purpose of securing and clarifying needed and vital information, such as discovering the needs that lie behind the numbers. The objective should not be to score debating points, alienate your alter negotiator, or make her defensive.

When you begin with the end in mind,
you gain a different perspective.
— Stephen Covey

64 Learn the language of hidden meanings.

Everything we say (and do) has a meaning. In a negotiation, where information is purposefully controlled and feigned, much of that meaning is lost to the unskilled and unwary negotiator.

Most people habitually, therefore unthinkingly, use words or phrases that mask the real meaning and intent of their communications. Some call this meta-talk, employing the word "meta" to imply a meaning that is beyond the obvious message. Meta-talk implies that the real, often intended, meaning is hidden from the unwary negotiator and that the truth is something other than the words alone would indicate. Optimal negotiators, ever in search of useful and pertinent information, listen for these telltale comments that can betray hidden but powerful and helpful meanings.

"I don't want to belabour the point, but ..." is an excellent illustration of meta-talk. Invariably, this statement signals the opposite intent — that what follows will be an embellishment on the point previously made. In the same vein, when your alter negotiator precedes a description of his thoughts with a phrase like "I was just thinking that ...", it's probable he has been thinking about the matter for awhile and this seems to be an appropriate opportunity to sneak it into the conversation. "Sneak" is an apt term. While some might suggest the phrasing to be diplomatic, meta-talk is little more than dishonest communication.

Meta-talk typically precedes an important part of the conversation. Should you not understand the real meaning of these innocuous phrases, it may prove injurious to your objective. If, as previously noted, a simple phrase like "off the top of my head" can actually mask a desire or intent to withhold a concession, then you have unwittingly based your decision to offer more on a false or misleading premise.

Meta-talk is a language of multiple meanings. So you need some tools to identify the truth behind these seemingly harmless words. We all use forms of meta-talk in social discourse, in the workplace and as gender or culture-specific terminology. Interpreting meta-talk requires an understanding of the communication nuances in these different arenas. Since it is habitual, pay attention also to the behavioural patterns of the speaker and to voice inflection.

The best way to recognize meta-talk in others is to acknowledge it in your own style of communication. Listen to the way you express yourself at moments when you are not being direct, as when you're trying to be subtle, overly polite or diplomatic. This will provide clues about what to listen for when others speak.

People will support the outcomes they help to create.

65   All of you is communicating.

Research tells us that non-verbal gestures account for most of the meaning in our communications. In a negotiation, the significance of body language is even more pronounced.

The study of non-verbal communication originated with Charles Darwin in the late 1800's and has been refined and confirmed by numerous studies since. The message for negotiators is this: our movements, postures and gestures can reveal one story while our voices are telling another. We are aware of what we are saying as we choose the words we want to speak and select the appropriate tone of voice to ensure the proper emphasis is conveyed. But we are not as conscious of the accompanying non-verbal cues we emit.

Many non-verbal behaviours cross cultures and some are universal in nature. Others are culture-specific. This includes gender – ever notice that most men put on their coats right arm first while women tend to put them on left arm first? Because non-verbal behaviour is learned, it is an unthinking habit for most. Therein lies its power in providing useful information and revealing insights into a negotiator's unexpressed attitudes and desires.

Like any language, non-verbal movements represent a complex communications process that consists of signals and cues as well as punctuation. A solitary gesture in isolation from other signals can be meaningless. More is better than less. Since body language is largely involuntary, it rarely lies about our true feelings. The perceptive communicator seeks to match non-verbal messages

All of you is communicating.

with verbal expressions of interest and intent.

We are more adept at reading body language than we realize. And women are usually better at it than men. It's as if we were blessed with a fail-safe mechanism that registers "tilt" whenever we receive a series of incongruent non-verbal messages.

Optimal negotiators take this understanding to a higher level by studying offensive and defensive body language maneuvers that complement their negotiating skills. This knowledge not only enables them to better detect the subtle but real meanings in communications but also equips them to use their own non-verbal gestures to advantage.

While there exists a large and fascinating body of literature, the best way to detect and better understand the meaning and purpose of non-verbal cues is simply to observe people interacting with others while endeavouring to discern what their intentional or unintentional signals really mean. This knowledge should be used as an asset rather than the liability it is for many unskilled negotiators.

What we obtain too cheap, we esteem too lightly.
– Thomas Paine

66

A tactic perceived is no tactic.

 Once a tactic has been identified and understood, it loses its inherent potential to cause pressure, physiological discomfort or psychological damage.

A tactic is any behaviour that is consciously or unconsciously intended to induce stress within your opponent. It is most effective when covert or implied. Consider this example: a longstanding member of your staff asks for some of your time to discuss a problem that's causing him some grief. After listening to his tale of woe, you readily see how bothersome the issue really is. His body language indicates a high degree of emotional upset, bordering on tears. Sensing this, you feel compassion and seek to alleviate your employee's distress. You suggest that he "take the rest of the day off" to regain his composure and perhaps, if appropriate, the discussion can be resumed at a more convenient time.

What if, unbeknownst to you, this same employee had told a colleague a few minutes before entering your office: "Watch this. The boss hates to see her staff upset about anything. She's especially a sucker for tears." In other words, the display of emotions to which you responded in kindness or compassion and apparent understanding was no more than a convenient set-up – a tactic deliberately conceived and executed according to his plan. Not knowing his tactic, you became his unwitting victim. Worse, you reinforced this Machiavellian behaviour by rewarding him with a day off work.

On the other hand, were you sufficiently perceptive to see his manipulation of your caring for others (a function of your own

131

A tactic perceived is no tactic.

self-concept and needs), you would likely have reacted differently. Though tempted, you would not have exposed the tactic, thereby creating an adrenal opponent. Rather, you would have waited for his emotional demonstration to subside. Then you would engage him in a more constructive discussion of solutions, with artful questions like "What do you think we can do to address this situation?"

Seeing manipulative behaviours and emotional ploys as tactics will enable you to become more perceptive, lower your stress and think of more tactically astute and intelligent responses.

In bargaining, virtually every behaviour should be viewed as a tactic designed to gain an advantage of some kind. Once they are identified and understood, their tactics become your opportunities to take control of the negotiation.

When one party gets something for nothing, the other usually gets nothing for something.

67 Leverage the power of your team.

Teams have certain advantages over individual negotiators, depending on the importance and complexity of the negotiation as well as the time available. They also have disadvantages. Know the difference.

A team approach offers a synergistic partnership with people who have different perspectives, expertise and experiences. This larger knowledge and perceptual base can be a distinct advantage in complex negotiations such as collective bargaining, international diplomacy and corporate acquisitions. Unlike going it on your own, teams ensure a pooling of judgements which enhance planning and allow for role specialization.

As a team leader, you need to ensure that everyone is given a vital, designated task to perform. These specified roles might include those of listener, note-taker or observer of non-verbal cues. Someone who is not focussed on a specific task can easily become a liability.

When more people are involved in the negotiating process as a team, there is greater commitment, more internal support and less stress. Tactically, teams can be used to offset a larger opposition group, enable legitimate delays (to caucus, for example), or create and leverage "bad guy, good guy" opportunities.

On the other hand, negotiating alone also has its advantages. Since complete authority is vested in one person, positions are not weakened through differences of opinion and questions cannot be aimed at weaker members to intentionally create disagreements among the team. Individual negotiators need not spend time sorting out competing interests and differences among team members. Rather, their focus is on making situational decisions to gain opportunistic concessions.

The real power of a team lies in its members seeing things differently. Deviants generate creativity. Good ideas come from seemingly unreasonable people who challenge accepted solutions, positions and norms.

Be mindful of team dynamics. Leverage your team's capabilities but don't capitulate to obstructionists. Don't give them an audience or reinforce difficult behaviour. Use deflection skills and move the discussion to the hallway when dealing with their agendas. Involve the passives (people who usually speak volumes at the wrong time). Never take silence for granted. Clear up all contentious points or potential areas of disagreement prior to the negotiation.

All power is a compound of time and patience.

68   Choose your team carefully.

 A bargaining team is like an orchestra. It must perform in harmony with each member reading from the same song sheet and none more important than the rest.

The designation of key roles and the co-ordination of the team's collective skills and talent can be the difference between making beautiful music together or generating conflicting noises and confusion.

In selecting team members and in assigning their roles, two objectives are paramount. First and foremost, the attributes of the person should match the role she is to perform. Second, everyone must understand the purpose of his particular role in the process. It helps if team members are compatible (in terms of their personalities, shared needs and objectives). Since this is rarely the case, effort must be directed to ensuring role/goal clarity, orchestration and focus.

Effective teams require a number of essential roles. There must be a leader/manager. If everyone's in charge, no one's in charge. The leader should be the only person who can announce concessions, call a caucus, make commitments or close. The leader is typically the spokesperson for the team (you should have only one), although this task can be assigned to an expert communicator. Team management implies responsibility for everything from logistics to team cohesion and discipline.

Teams enable the inclusion of experts whose knowledge is pertinent to achieving the desired objectives. Experts should only speak on their areas of expertise (remember, experts like to

Choose your team carefully.

talk). A scribe is critical as notes are needed to work out discrepancies and to structure the final agreement. The meeting notes should be yours, not theirs. (Be careful about making over-commitments as everything is recorded.) Note-takers can also strategically pace the process. The scribe's power invariably increases over time.

If numbers permit, having one member of your team focus his attention on the dynamics of the process is advisable. He watches the body language, listens to the meta-talk, catches inadvertent signals and gauges the climate.

Another luxury that accompanies negotiating in teams is the opportunity to include a deviant – a team member who purposefully takes the other side's position. In caucus, she assumes the role of "devil's advocate" and adds value to the strategy by recommending appropriate phrasing and timing of proposals to enhance acceptance.

*Confidence comes not from always being right
but from not fearing to be wrong.
– Peter T. McIntyre*

69 Team size matters.

 Determining the optimum size of your negotiating team is an important strategic consideration. Size should be an advantage, not a liability.

The ideal number of team members should be tempered by a cost-benefit assessment of both internal and external factors. Having an odd number of members reduces the likelihood of deadlocks within the team, especially when determining alternative or contentious tactics. However, groups of three can generate problems if two members consistently form a coalition and seek to dominate the other team member. Coalition formation in even-numbered groups is also possible and can produce deadlocks. It helps to establish ground rules for avoiding such impasses.

The advantages of larger teams (four or more members) are that they can plan more thoroughly, set higher goals, consume more time (when necessary), afford greater role/task specialization and, assuming team solidarity, develop greater emotional stability, heightened creativity and work well under stress.

Conversely, teams that are too large have inherent disadvantages. They can be difficult to assemble and schedule, consensus formation is either unlikely or difficult, irrelevant agendas and comments are frequently introduced which prolong negotiations, and there is a greater need for peer approval.

Larger teams can also waste a lot of time and effort, require more time and skill to manage, have a tendency to include some dead weight and can obviously be more costly. Whether

Team size matters.

an advantage or a disadvantage, compared to individual negotiators, larger teams do tend to take greater risks.

The advantages of smaller teams (three or fewer members) are that they produce quicker results, plan more efficiently, use limited agency more effectively, can defer to absent experts and avoid questions about same, use time tactics more adeptly and are more economical.

The potential disadvantages of small teams include the possibility of perceived intimidation in the presence of larger groups, the probable lack of needed expertise, and the absence of appropriate role players, when these are required.

These minimal considerations should help you to determine the size of a team that will best serve your objectives.

I have never in my life learned anything
from any man who agreed with me.
— Dudley Field Malone

Price is a
point of view.

 Price is the value ascribed by the seller. Understanding the reason for that value must be a primary objective for the buyer.

There are places in the world where price tags don't exist. That's because the true value of the item being offered for sale, the price at which it will sell, is known only by the buyer. Because what he might be prepared to pay for an item he desires or even covets is likely more than the seller might ever think of asking.

At the outset of a negotiation, we are often unduly influenced by the price that is asked. We fail to think of the price as little more than an expression of what the seller hopes the article might be worth to a willing buyer. Also, obviously, an experienced negotiator will build in a cushion to provide sufficient latitude to ensure his objective is achieved.

If we concur with the ask price, we should have no qualms about paying it. However, if we disagree with the price, for whatever reason, we should have no difficulty negotiating for a more acceptable price (one more in line with our own perception of value). The objective is not to change the price by "haggling the numbers" but, first, to seek to understand the point of view behind the number and, then, to proceed to change it.

Words (or numbers) that appear in print have a power that affects attitudes and behaviour. This is one reason why people who check into hotels invariably leave either at or before the

Price is a point of view.

time indicated on a little sign posted somewhere in the room. Likewise, consumers may refuse to return unsatisfactory merchandise when there's a printed sign above a cash register that reads "All sales final." These instructions or rules, on analysis, are little more than the express preferences of management who, for the sake of its own convenience, would like you to leave the hotel by a prescribed hour or who don't want to deal with the hassle of returning your (possibly used) purchases to their shelves.

To be successful in negotiations, do not focus your discussion on the price, the policy or the words and numbers printed on signs, in employment manuals or in contracts. Rather, concentrate your efforts on discovering the reasons why those who seek protection from such printed documents hold those views.

Consider how your approach to negotiating will change when you start seeing these defenses differently. Don't take them for granted and don't take them literally. You're not challenging a price tag; you're discussing the reasons behind a "point-of-view tag." You're not disrespecting the policy; you simply want to know why it exists and why it applies to you in this instance. When you do this, when you challenge without debating the numbers, your aspiration level and ability to persuade rise exponentially.

The bitterness of poor quality lingers
long after the sweetness of cheap price is forgotten.

71

Price and terms are symbiotic.

Developing and using terms and conditions creatively will enable you to negotiate anything, with anyone.

"Price" is the most visible component of the total cost in any negotiation. The conditions and specifications that comprise the rest of the items being negotiated can have differing values but rarely are they the primary focus in most negotiations. The relationship between price and terms is mutually beneficial. Hence, acceptable trade-offs can always be found. My purpose is to satisfy your needs by building a package of terms that enables or motivates you to reconsider your price.

Conversely, I can agree to your initial position on price and, in exchange, request terms that either undermine or cast doubt on the security of the price. If you seek better, more acceptable terms relative to your needs, your only leverage in convincing me would be to alter your price.

Some people naively think they can have both price and terms. That is illogical. Were it not so, then the first condition asked would be to insist on quadrupling the price. And, if that were the case, the higher price would have been your opening position. Since you can't have both (price and terms), your objective is to negotiate an acceptable mix of the two. This is the essence of bargaining.

The symbiotic relationship that exists between price and terms enables you to creatively leverage one against the other. As seller, it is advisable to begin by seeking acceptance of your price. When you feel you've achieved as much as possible, you

Price and terms are symbiotic.

then should ask for terms in a manner that presumes you will receive them. Should these not be readily forthcoming, you can use the failure to achieve satisfaction on your terms as a reason to reopen a discussion of the price.

Buyers, on the other hand, would work the price-terms equation in reverse. Since they are paying for the total package, they should open with a discussion of terms and then seek to minimize the price by taking away terms to which they seemingly have agreed.

The ability to leverage price and terms is directly dependent on the quality of your preparedness to negotiate. Optimal negotiators creatively develop terms, conditions and options that enable them to purposefully modify an adversary's opening position. They realize that the more bargaining chips they can put on the table, the better is their opportunity to create a package that "fits" the needs of both parties. Thus equipped, given the symbiotic relationship between price and terms, they know that any deal can be made.

Charm is a way of getting the answer yes
without asking a clear question.
- Albert Camus

72   Reinforce your opening.

 Your bargaining posture, or what you do in developing a concession pattern between your initial position and the closing, must reinforce the credibility of your opening.

Appropriate attention must be given to opening your negotiations realistically. The opening position (or number) should be phrased in such a way as to create, alter and otherwise diminish the other person's initial expectations. Movement from that point, through the timely offering of concessions, should be designed to reinforce the believability of your opening and thus your reputation as a negotiator. This subsequent giving of concessions, or bargaining posture, should be configured to convey a message of strength, not one of weakness or, worse, confusion.

Say, for example, that I want to sell my watch. My objective is to get $1,000. A good opening, one that raises expectations, might be to ask $1,500. I have a willing buyer who makes a reasonable initial offer. With the range of settlement established, I continue the discussion via a concession – I now lower my price to $1,400. The buyer expresses his interest in the watch by increasing his offer. It's my turn again. I respond by asking $1,250. The question is: am I exhibiting a strong or weak bargaining posture?

Quite obviously, it's weak. My concessions are getting larger, not smaller. I'm sending the wrong message. Worse, it's become clear to the buyer that my opening position was probably a "high ball." If ever I should do business with this buyer again, he may not take my openings seriously.

Reinforce your opening.

My concession pattern should be sending a different message, one that implies I don't have a lot of room left. But, clearly, my last concession belies that perception. A better counter offer would have been to reduce my asking price to perhaps $1,350. (And, should another still be required, to $1,337.)

A strong bargaining posture is achieved when each concession is a fraction of the one preceding it. What counts in negotiating is not the numbers you present but the message your alter negotiator derives from your concessions.

Observe how those with whom you negotiate make their concessions. You can tell a great deal about the veracity of their opening positions, and thus their credibility as negotiators, by assessing the bargaining posture against the initial number. These insights will enable you to anticipate and forecast future concessions. In your case, seek to ensure your concession pattern reinforces rather than undermines your opening position.

Know each other as if you were brothers;
negotiate deals as if you were strangers to each other.
- Arab Proverb

73 Deadlines are of your own making.

Optimal negotiators know every deadline is negotiable. The naive negotiator holds them to be sacrosanct. The latter feels the pressure; the former sees the opportunity.

Challenging the imposition of a deadline, even one that can be readily accommodated, can provide useful information about your negotiating latitude as well valuable insights into your adversary's bargaining style. Suppose you are given a deadline of midnight tonight to consummate an important commercial transaction. Your immediate response should be to test both the firmness of the deadline and the negotiator's resolve in holding you to it.

When you do this, be sure to give a plausible reason for not being able to cede to this seemingly rigid condition. Say something like, "I'm afraid I can't respond by midnight tonight. I have a family commitment that's very important to my son and he's counting on my being there for him. If you could just give me until tomorrow night, I could probably get back to you with something you might like."

The probability of getting an extension on the deadline is good. The issue is not whether he cares about disappointing your son – rather, it's that you have a reason for being unable to meet his deadline. And you did say your counter might be favourable. In addition to getting more time, you've discovered that your alter negotiator may also be flexible on other points in the negotiation.

Deadlines are of your own making.

Whether the reason for requesting an extension is valid or not is irrelevant. Why create pressure on yourself by accepting a time line that doesn't allow you to think through or investigate options and alternatives?

The majority of your concessions will be made at the "eleventh hour," that point immediately adjacent to the perceived deadline. If you are able to reduce the pressure inherent in a deadline, then capitalize on it.

Conversely, even when you don't have a deadline to meet, you should impose one just to create a sense of urgency and put added pressure on your alter negotiator. How he responds to that pressure will be instructive and could be beneficial.

Deadlines are an integral part of the negotiating process. That is why they too are negotiable. Depending upon whose deadline it is, plan for it. Think about what you'll say and do if the deadline is imposed. Deadlines are inevitable and unavoidable; so have an answer ready.

The success of tactics are commensurate with the amount of time invested in them.

74 When you don't know what to do, do nothing.

The most difficult thing to do when faced with uncertainty or pressure is to do nothing. It's also the best thing to do.

The ability to take a momentary pause when required is critical to your success. Its purpose is to enable you to think and then to take control ... of yourself. With this self-control comes the ability to control others.

If the fundamental purpose of a tactic is to induce stress, anxiety and confusion, the antidote is to have the presence of mind to get in touch with your own true feelings. As you pause, ask yourself why you're feeling tense, unsure or intimidated. This precious time-out is your opportunity to question why the other person is behaving as he is. When you stop and think, good answers are likely to follow.

A pregnant pause is a way of listening to yourself. A few seconds is sufficient to "get a grip" on what needs to be said or done. It also sends a powerful message, as silence is rare in most negotiations. The perception taken is usually one of appraisal – a contemplative gesture that rarely has negative connotations.

Josh Billings once said, "Silence is one of the hardest arguments to refute." Optimal negotiators understand his advice. Indeed, the best answers are sometimes the ones without words.

In getting comfortable with your own silence, you may need something on which to focus. Ask yourself some important questions. When words are spoken that cause you discomfort or confusion, there is usually a reason. In the heat of the

When you don't know what to do, do nothing.

exchange, you may be reacting to the words spoken or to the intonation of voice rather than the purpose behind them. So a good question to ask yourself at such an awkward moment would be: "Why is she saying that to me?"

Alternatively, as noted, get in touch with your feelings. Ask yourself why you're now feeling the way you do. Take stock of your own emotions and try to figure out what's causing your distress. Questions that enable you to focus on the cause and effect of her words can help you to think of more artful, intelligent and appropriate responses – ones designed to pinpoint motives, diffuse emotional counterattacks that unnecessarily escalate the conflict, and take back control of the discussion.

It has been observed that human beings are the only creatures on the face of the earth who can talk themselves into trouble. Properly timed silence will prevent that "foot-in-mouth" disease from spreading further.

> *It is better to keep your mouth shut and appear stupid*
> *than to open it and remove all doubt.*
> *– Samuel Clemens*

75   Always write the agreement.

If the agreement is to be formal, make sure you do the writing. Never leave the drafting to someone else's notes or memory, unless you want to support their wishful thinking.

A memorandum of agreement (or understanding) is a document drawn up after the negotiation that sets forth the commitments of each party and establishes the framework and key points of the settlement. When writing such an agreement, as you should, you need to keep a few basic points in mind.

It's good counsel to remember that whatever is written may ultimately be read in a court of law. Never try to quote the law (unless you're a lawyer). If it's in the law, it shouldn't be in your agreement. And laws occasionally change. So write accordingly.

Express the agreement in your language, as you understand it, such that it becomes the basis for any possible future revisions. Keep the language precise and concise. A preamble isn't necessary as extra language only creates the possibility for loopholes and subsequent misinterpretation.

If they say they will write the agreement, tell them you will do your own draft for comparison purposes. This means the negotiation is not over and has just entered a different phase. A further benefit of offering to do this task is that inexperienced negotiators may be appreciative and thus perhaps tend not to quibble over lesser points.

Always write the agreement.

Eliminate statements of philosophy, especially if it happens to be your own. Unless you purposefully want to subsequently broaden the scope of negotiations, avoid reference to secondary documents (however relevant they may seem to be). If you have doubts about the commitments made, use cautionary language like "whenever possible" or "when feasible."

If advantageous or prudent, endeavour to have the other person initial key clauses or the pages of the agreement. Suggest that it's only a formality to ensure "we don't go back over points already agreed." The purpose is to lock in agreement whenever possible.

Once you've drafted the agreement, leave it for a day or "sleep on it" before sending it back to the other party. Go over the agreement once more and have someone who has not been involved in the negotiation proofread the document for accuracy. You may not get a second chance to correct an innocent typo, misplaced emphasis or forgotten understanding.

Every human benefit and enjoyment, every virtue,
every prudent act is founded on barter and compromise.
— Edmund Burke

76

Exceptions
disprove the rule.

 There is no such thing as a general rule. The law of averages does not prevail in negotiating. The fact that "everyone is doing it" doesn't mean you must do it as well.

Artful negotiating is creating or encouraging exceptions to the rules. Were this not the case, you would logically expect to be treated the same way as everyone else. And whoever sets the rules would rule your behaviour.

If your alter negotiator pressures you by saying that "the average selling price" (*e.g.*, for houses in a particular neighbourhood) is below what you have asked, then the onus is on you to indicate why your asking price is an exception to the marketplace norm. Your challenge lies in making a convincing case to support your contention that a higher price should prevail. As always, your advantage will flow from probing the needs of the buyer – why does he want to buy this particular house? That, and that alone, will determine the price he is willing to pay.

People usually ascribe a value to what they seek and rarely is it entirely a function of what industry averages, professional standards or "the marketplace" might otherwise suggest. The price they are willing to pay is a consequence of their unique needs, interests, motives and aspirations.

The use of terms like professional standards and common practices is no more than a tactic designed to reduce your hopes and expectations of a better outcome. Averages and aggregates minimize exceptions. To illustrate, no one could comprehend the media reports of the untimely death of the hiker in the woods who drowned while forging a stream that was, on average, only two feet deep. This average, of course, also accounted for the 20 foot hole in the middle.

In the same vein, be wary of the use of statistics. They too do not prove the validity of averages. Always question the sample used to support the data. When three out of four dentists recommend a particular brand of toothpaste, which four dentists are we talking about? Are they the same ones one receive complimentary cases of the product for their patients? If so, might not the recommendation, albeit persuasive, be biased?

Whenever statistics are used for comparison purposes, ensure it's an "apples to apples" application. Then, if need be, focus on the exceptional or extraordinary circumstances that support your position.

The exclusive use of force eventually raises up
the forces that destroy it.
— Anatol Rappoport

77 Promote your credibility.

Optimal negotiators understand the art of and the need for self-promotion. They enhance their credibility by merchandising their success.

The day you stop promoting yourself and your interests is the day you stop advancing. Opportunities don't always go to the most qualified but to those who promote themselves the best and who are in the right place at the right time. This may seem unfair but it is not entirely accidental. To advance your cause, keep looking for the right place and time. Seek out or create opportunities that position and communicate your value.

Today, in business especially, we talk a lot about "value added." Value that isn't perceived and measurable, isn't added. Never doubt your value at the negotiating table. Find ways to demonstrate it in terms that are appreciated and understood by the other party. This will add immensely to your power base. When value is perceived, influence follows. That's when people listen and are persuaded.

The venerable journalist, Edward R. Murrow, offers this sage counsel: "To be persuasive, you must be believable. To be believable, you must be credible. To be credible, you must be truthful." Optimal negotiators practice that dictum.

The repetition of a persuasive and credible position or message inevitably leads to acceptance. Use different words to restate the same position. Remember the importance of appropriate phrasing to induce desired perceptions.

Promote your credibility.

Effective self-promotion depends on continuously demonstrated self-improvement. Getting better in all that you do is critical to your power and success as a negotiator. Without a verifiable track record, you cannot sell yourself to others and, thus, you cannot sell your point of view.

Credible self-promotion requires an understanding of your own needs and values. Knowing what's really important in your life will make a discernable difference in your negotiations. When you are clear about what you want (as well as what you don't want) to achieve, the expectation of positive outcomes becomes self-affirming and self-fulfilling. Thinking that you will do well, in effect by believing your own self-promotion, can literally pull you towards that end.

One must learn by doing the thing; for though you think you know it you have no certainty until you try.
— Sophocles

78 Negotiate with decision makers.

 Don't negotiate seriously with someone who lacks the authority to make the deal unless you enjoy wasting your time.

A negotiator who lacks this authority is known as a limited agent. As the words suggest, the mandate to negotiate a deal is limited to that which is determined by the decision maker. Skillful negotiators who work in sophisticated bargaining arenas, such as union-management negotiations or international diplomacy, often use limited agents to reduce the number of issues and collect important information. They know that their ability to make a final decision, whether bestowed by title or power, can be a disadvantage at the bargaining table. So others are called upon to perform that role.

When in the presence of a limited agent, optimal negotiators honour the role. They understand that agents are often given the power to settle provided it is within their mandate, which rarely are they authorized to exceed. They appreciate that this designated individual can be an asset – an influencer – when the time comes to move the negotiations "upstairs" where the real decision maker resides.

Never go around limited agents; go through them. Despite the frustration that may accompany the effort, aligning with the needs and interests of the agent can be a smart strategy. Having been given an untenable mandate, she may well have the same problem as you. At an appropriate time, outline the benefits of together taking the problem to the higher court of the decision maker.

Negotiate with decision makers.

In some cases, the decision at the higher level to accept or reject a position is made by a group, typically through some kind of voting mechanism. In this scenario, the agent's observations and recommendation may carry greater weight. In such cases, your primary focus should be on helping the agent sell the agreement to his constituency.

Limited agents will sometimes feign their authority, suggesting that it is greater than it actually is. They falsely assume this might help them make a better deal. The more explicit this claim, the less it should be believed.

Most agents, when pressed artfully, will reveal their constraints – especially when their restricted mandate gives them a sense of security. And often because they are "just trying to do their job." This is an opportunity to align with their needs by validating their role and their effort to reach a sustainable agreement which will reflect well on their reputation.

Only decision makers can make binding agreements. Limited agents might get you closer to that settlement opportunity but they are clearly not in a position to optimize the deal.

Why should I question the monkey
when I can question the monkey grinder?
– Aneurin Bevan

79   Humanize yourself.

 First impressions are lasting impressions. The key to winning lies in the ability to establish rapport with the other negotiator.

It doesn't take long to make an indelible impression. The dynamic initial seconds and minutes of an encounter can be crucial to the future of a relationship, let alone the outcome of a negotiation. Although we simultaneously project and receive important signals, rarely are we aware of the significance of our words and our body language in establishing and maintaining that vital first assessment.

Optimal negotiators understand the significant tactical advantages that accrue from personal alignment. Rapport is the basis of trust and, when people trust you, they usually tell you what you need to know. They give you quality information. We align with those who appear to understand our needs. And we are more persuasive when we can deliver our message in words that appeal to their needs, not ours. We must therefore endeavour to translate ourselves as much as our words.

Translation acknowledges that no two people speak the same "language." Each of us speaks with our own unique variations of an ostensibly common vocabulary. Consider the dialogue of the deaf that can ensue between parent and teenager – the same words may be used but the meanings are quite different.

We often use words imprecisely and rely on pet phrases, jargon and acronyms. Our language is a reflection of our own individual "culture." Effective translation requires us to listen to the

Humanize yourself.

other person's language before we can communicate our ideas in words they understand. Not only do they better understand the words, they assimilate them more readily and may be genuinely motivated by our message.

Establishing rapport requires both non-verbal and verbal communication. How we dress and behave, our mannerisms and gestures, can all convey our "likeability" and intent. We tend to accept and align with people who appear similar to ourselves. The most important gesture in encouraging alignment is giving a spontaneous, genuine smile and making eye contact. Those who avert their gaze are perceived as lacking credibility. Worse, it can convey an impression of submissiveness or guilt.

To create a positive impression, use open-ended questions. Most people like to talk about themselves. So encourage them to do so, especially during that critical first meeting. The more you allow people to talk about themselves, the more they will like you. In a casual and subtle way, lean towards the other person. This supportive posture tells them you are interested in what they have to say. Lastly, names are important to some people. Get them on first meeting people, get them right and use them often.

A thick skin can be a gift from God.
— Konrad Adenauer

80 Trade expendables to achieve essentials.

 Negotiating is about trade-offs. Giving gets. Since people have different needs, endeavour to exchange things that don't matter a great deal to you for those that do.

Unskilled negotiators fail by limiting their objectives to, and by focusing their attention on, those things they absolutely must have. After defining a minimum number of wants, they enter the negotiation inadequately prepared. For them, these essential core needs are the only requirements that must be satisfied. Giving these up is tantamount to losing.

Expendables are synonymous with maximum objectives. These are the things you do not require in order to satisfy your primary needs. While it should be made to appear (by your words and actions) that you do need them, they are clearly intended as negotiable. The greater the number of expendables you take into a negotiation, the better is your ability to structure a package that will be acceptable to your adversary.

Expendables are the "bargaining chips" you can afford to lose without violating your "must haves." The added benefit is that some of your expendables will not be of interest to the other party. Thus, just by asking, they too can easily become yours.

Inventive negotiators prepare by creatively developing as long a list of objectives as they possibly can, several of which they fully intend to "concede." Negotiations are viewed primarily as opportunities and, as such, in their planning they purposefully become wishful thinkers. They reflect as much on what they need to acquire as on what might fortuitously come their way.

Trade expendables to achieve essentials.

All concessions, regardless of their relative importance on your expendables list, should be given away slowly and reluctantly. At least they must be so perceived by your alter negotiator. The more begrudgingly, if not painfully, these concessions are perceived to be given, the greater will be your opponent's sense of elation and victory. For that too is a primary objective in conveying a win-win feeling.

Your purpose must not only be to ensure that the other person wins something but also that he thinks he took something from you that you did not want to give. You cannot get unless you first give. But, artfully, ensure that what you give is not what you need to have. Protect your essentials by ensuring a sufficient number of appealing expendables.

To get to the promised land, you must negotiate
your way through the wilderness.

81 If it seems "too good," it probably is.

In negotiations, as in life, you reap what you sow. Return on investment (of time, effort and creativity) is the name of the game. Rarely, if ever, can you get something for nothing.

Those things that come to you too easily or too early should always be suspect. People don't freely give away things of value unless they are extremely naive or have ulterior motives. The adage "you get what you pay for" is certainly relevant in making good deals.

Negotiating to optimize the outcome is a deliberate building-block process. It requires considerable patience and inventiveness before the other person will change her point of view or alter convictions that are deeply held. To be appreciated, deals need time to develop, mature and ripen.

Consider also that your own satisfaction with an agreement made too easily is likely to be fleeting. What if you approached me with an opening offer of $5,000 for something I wanted to sell. In an instant, I say "OK, take it ... it's yours." Would you be happy with my response? I doubt it. What if, after several hours of haggling the price, you got it but for several hundred dollars more? Would you be happier? I think so.

It's human nature to prize more highly those things that are earned and especially those things that are gained through one's own skill, knowledge and experience. Without this investment of effort and ingenuity, haunting second doubts typically arise after the deal has been consummated. This

If it seems "too good," it probably is.

remorse is often articulated with such self-criticism as "perhaps I could have done better, if only ...."

Negotiating, properly done, requires an investment of time and effort. It is typically an emotional roller coaster. The sensation of highs and lows before the end of the ride is to be expected. Indeed, the enjoyment of the experience is the sum of the parts.

The realization that the deal might be "too good to be true" should come at the end of the process, not at the beginning. And it must be as a consequence of your expertise as a negotiator, not the perceived largesse of the other party.

When someone sells you "something for nothing," don't bother reading the warranty. It isn't worth the paper it's printed on.

The most effective action both resorts to power and engages conscience.
— Barbara Deming

82 Acknowledge gender differences.

 Men and women negotiate differently. Cultural awareness and a sensitivity towards dissimilar negotiating styles must also factor in these differences in gender.

Our socialization produces different behavioural orientations. Men are naturally more competitive than women, a consequence of playing on sports teams or at war games during formative years. Men were taught how to suit up, knock heads and go for a beer after the game. Men like to compete and win, especially when they can revel in their own performance. That makes men good win-lose negotiators, where the object is usually winning at the expense of the other party.

Women, on the other hand, are more collaborative by nature, tending to look for the fair play and equity in encounters with others. They are also more likely to personalize conflict. They don't like knocking heads and the last person they would ever want to have a beer with is someone who assaults them verbally in an accusing or aggressive way. In general, not surprisingly, women make better win-win negotiators.

These are neither pejorative nor chauvinistic comments. Nor is one negotiating style necessarily superior to the other – it all depends on the circumstances and the objectives. But these differences in style and approach should not be taken for granted; rather, with awareness, they can be used to advantage. While these tendencies are based on sound research, they ought not lead to stereotypical, knee-jerk responses. Both men and women can exhibit the primary gender traits of the other.

Acknowledge gender differences.

Beyond cultural or sociological differences that effect style, men and women possess different strengths when it comes to mirroring optimal negotiating attributes.

Women, who are by nature more relationship focussed, are better than men at reading body language. They are more perceptive when it comes to discerning subtle micro-gestures – the almost imperceptible but nonetheless telltale signs that can amplify the real meaning behind a feigned message. Men, who are more task focussed by nature, are likely to miss these signals and thus to read the message literally.

Since half of your negotiations are probably with people of the opposite sex, make these gender differences work for you rather than against you.

*The secret to walking on water
is knowing where the stones are.*

83   Listen for telltale traps.

 Listening is an essential skill in every negotiator's arsenal. But if you don't know what you're listening for, you may find yourself caught in a thinking trap.

When negotiators overuse superlatives in describing their offers, positions or wants, they are usually hiding something that is worthy of probing further. While everything may be a matter of degree, exaggerations should be viewed as red flags that signal danger zones. Dissect hyperbole by asking pointer questions: When he says, "I just can't go that high," you should be asking "How high could you go?" If your alter negotiator uses words like always or never, dig deeper into the meaning with a probing response such as "Always?"

In a negotiation, every statement must be considered a point of view. In other words, it's biased. Never accept a point of view as constituting a fact. Acknowledge and label it for what it is. Beware as well when statistics are used to justify positions. Keep in mind Mark Twain's advice that statistics are often little more than lies. While they can be powerfully seductive, statistics are invariably self-serving. Question the relevance of the data to your situation.

Slogans and motherhood statements can have a calming effect that belie their real purpose. Phrases like 'fair and reasonable,' 'you get what you pay for,' and 'everything's going up these days' are typically used to disarm or undermine your reservations. The skillful presumption, and thus the trap, is that your circumstances (and therefore your position) are analogous to the conditions implied in such statements.

Listen for telltale traps.

An example does not constitute proof even though that may be your alter negotiator's intention. Pay attention when you hear the words "for example" and be prepared to refute evidence offered in the guise of false proof.

Likewise, a single incident does not create a generalization or rule of thumb. Be on guard for true or seemingly profound statements that neither prove anything nor add value to the discussion. These can also serve as signals that a trap is about to be set.

We can all become the unwitting victims of our biases and prejudices, our wants and needs. It's human nature to believe what we want to believe, especially when it confirms our self-image. While it may be difficult, be wary of attempts to play on your ego needs. If she says, "You're one hell of a good negotiator," acknowledge the flattery then refocus the conversation. "Thank you. Now about our problem ...."

*It isn't where you've been,
it's where you're going that matters most.*

84

Say "yes" when you're happy.

There is no accepted formula for determining that which makes a good deal. Its meaning is unique to every negotiator. Whatever makes you happy constitutes, and should be accepted as, a good deal.

Happiness is a relative concept. What makes you happy and what makes another person happy are matters of individual perception and feelings. Measuring one's hopes and desires against artificial benchmarks or the expectations of others is counterproductive and debilitating to your self-esteem. What counts is you – your own expectations of performance and the inner peace and joy that accompany what you sense is a winning experience.

Some negotiators endeavour to gain considerably more than the achievement of their primary objectives. In the pursuit of sometimes impossible gains, they succeed only in creating a deadlock. Furthermore, in seeking this elusive higher goal, they feel compelled to offer more than they really want to give. They fail to appreciate the truism that, in negotiating, there can always be "another day" – an opportunity to go back to the table and try again.

An advertisement directed at those who drink and drive can also have sobering insights for negotiators. It ends with the following advice: "That one for the road can kill you." It follows that your purpose as a negotiator is sometimes to take your gains in hand and live to fight another day. The only thing certain about most negotiations is that they inevitably lead to another negotiation.

Say "yes" when you're happy.

Never let your ego get in the way of your negotiating objectives; focus on achieving a settlement today, one that gives you personal satisfaction in the accomplishment, while creating an even better opportunity for tomorrow. When you're satisfied with the deal before you, say "yes."

While this judgement is always yours to make, some things ought not be negotiable. Your principles for starters. If the deal cannot be made without you having to compromise your fundamental values, rethink the deal. In other words, when you don't feel good about the deal, don't make it. Trust your instincts. Regroup and plan for the next encounter.

You have to expect things of yourself before you can do them.
— Michael Jordan

85   Risk taking is its own reward.

A risk is not a 50/50 proposition. Though there is invariably a downside consequence, the odds are usually in your favour. And success depends on where you choose to focus your attention.

Poor risk takers are those who view a 90% probability of success as a risk not worth taking. They would rather focus their attention on the 10% possibility of failure and be dissuaded from proceeding. Their analysis of what might go wrong, rather than what might go right, prevents them from venturing forth to try new things – challenging and exploring the possibilities and seeing problems as opportunities.

Risk is typically a 60/40 proposition, meaning that there is a 60% probability of success and a 40% chance of failure. Anything less than that probably wouldn't make it onto our cautious adult radar screen of risks. While the odds may be in your favour, the question is always whether the trade-off is justified or acceptable.

Optimal negotiators understand that the reward or the return on investment is proportionate to the risk. For them, a .600 (and certainly a .900) batting average is pretty impressive. And, having done the necessary homework, their risk taking is well thought out and calculated rather than a cavalier, daring leap into the unknown.

Beyond the power and the potential that resides in taking risks, there is another reward worth considering. Whether we succeed or fail, risk taking is a great teacher. We learn far more from

Risk taking is its own reward.

our failures than our successes. We dwell painfully on the former, and thereby learn from the experience, while taking the latter more or less for granted. When we fail, we tend to contemplate the reasons why and we don't move on as quickly as when we succeed.

This critical reflection and invaluable self-discovery is often referred to as learning from the school of hard knocks. There is value in trial and error. We look back on failed risks and, contemplating the "could haves" and "should haves" of alternative strategies and decisions, grow from the experience. Adversity strengthens character.

Seen in this light, while risk taking is a source of power at the negotiating table, it is also an invaluable opportunity to learn about oneself and to discover what works and what doesn't. If you don't try, you will never know. Should you try and fail, you will have become a better negotiator for the experience.

If you don't ask for it, you won't get it.
Test, challenge and explore the possibilities.

86 Heed the 90:10 rules.

 A vital key to negotiating success lies in the ability to discern useful information from that intended to confuse, mislead or disarm.

Since information is the ultimate source of power in a negotiation, there are two basic 90:10 "rules" you need to know. First, much like an iceberg, 90% of what you need to discover in a negotiation likely lies below the surface. It is your responsibility, through good planning, perseverance and skillful questioning, to dive beneath that surface and to unearth quality information that is either consciously or unknowingly being feigned, concealed or withheld.

While the 90:10 principle is a concept for illustration purposes, in complex negotiations, the equation is not necessarily an understatement. Solid questioning and good listening skills are critical to success. The next time you view your alter negotiator, think iceberg. Focus on bringing to the surface the huge amount of potentially invaluable information that can make a difference in generating a more favourable outcome.

The second 90:10 rule is just as important. Ninety percent of what you hear in a negotiation is likely nonsense, superfluous and intended to mislead you. In crass terms, it's just utter "BS" designed to obfuscate and disguise the more critical information. Focus your attention, through artful communication skills, on discovering the 10% that can truly make a difference. Become a detective. Look for clues to deceit and ferret out what you need to know.

Heed the 90:10 rules.

To mix metaphors, the objective of a negotiation is to distinguish wheat from chaff and then get to "the meat" of the matter. Don't be confused or disarmed by specious or gratuitous remarks. Find those vital pieces of pertinent information that enable you to discern genuine needs from wants and build a package that can and will serve the needs of both parties.

These two simple principles can help you prepare better and focus your tactics. Minimally, they will help to improve your efficiency as a negotiator.

People love to buy. They just hate to be sold.

87

You have to enjoy it to be good.

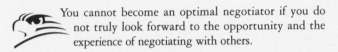 You cannot become an optimal negotiator if you do not truly look forward to the opportunity and the experience of negotiating with others.

Most people understand how to negotiate. Unfortunately, they often lack the motivation to do it. Despite a seemingly endless number of wonderful opportunities to better their cause and station in life, they are intimidated by the encounter. This lack of enthusiasm for the chance to prevail in a contest of skills, wills and minds impairs their capacity to satisfy needs, get ahead in life and achieve true happiness.

The art of negotiation is an escape from the ordinary, the routine and the boring. It is a means of getting what you want and an essential method of doing business. It can be an exciting, pleasurable activity offering the challenge and rewards that accompany the resolution of difficult problems. It produces a sensation of being alert and quick of wit.

Negotiating enables us to learn about human behaviour and grow with the knowledge that we can overcome barriers and master complex situations. Skilled negotiators are respected for their persuasiveness and benefit personally by developing skills that reinforce a positive self-image. The team effort required in some negotiations produces an appreciation of others and an enduring bond of camaraderie.

There is no area of human endeavour that equates to the satisfaction of convincing others. The ability to do so can immeasurably enhance the quality of your life and the lives of

You have to enjoy it to be good.

the important people around you. The thrill of victory and agony of defeat are character builders that last a lifetime. Given such extraordinary benefits, how could you not enjoy negotiating?

The objective of negotiating with others is to ensure they "buy into" and support the moral, ethical or economic validity of your positions and the rightness of your point of view. The mastery of this critical skill is founded principally on a genuine desire to do it, and do it well.

The purpose of becoming an optimal negotiator is to achieve personal happiness. Supported by acquired knowledge, skills and understanding, that quest is a journey worth relishing.

The ability to determine the quality of one's own life is the highest of skills.

88 These things you NEVER do.

The purpose of this companion is to provide you with appropriate wisdom, simple advice and expert guidance on what to do in your negotiations and how to consummate significantly better deals.

These are principles and prescriptions, borne of considerable practical experience, that can enhance your winning percentage.

In closing, optimal negotiators also know that there are some important things you just never do – things that are counterproductive to achieving your objectives and, worse, that may harm your reputation. Such as ....

Never tell the other person how much further you might have gone. (Because you will make them feel like a loser and losers always seek to even the score, however long that may take.)

Never openly expose or otherwise indicate that you understand their tactics. (Because it's better to negotiate with thinking opponents, not adrenal, irrational or defensive adversaries.)

Never enter a negotiation without having creative alternatives in mind. (Because, when you have no options, you always pay top dollar.)

Never tell a lie about something that can subsequently be revealed or proven to the contrary. (Because your reputation is more important than any victory, no matter how large. And, as you've discovered, you can win without being dishonest.)

These things you NEVER do.

Never bargain in bad faith. (Because the sweet taste of a good deal will be significantly diminished.)

Never compromise your principles. (Because the only person you must spend the rest of your life with is you.)

Never leave home for an important negotiation without taking along your annotated copy of The **optimal** *negotiator*. (Because it is a companion that can serve you well in deals yet to be made.)

It is funny about life: if you refuse to accept anything
but the very best you will very often get it.
— W. Somerset Maugham

The Author

Jim Murray has been researching, teaching and practicing the art of negotiating for over 30 years. Not surprisingly, he has direct experience in virtually every negotiating arena ranging from complex commercial transactions and collective bargaining to corporate acquisitions and international peacekeeping. He has been publicly hailed "a negotiator's negotiator" by one of Canada's foremost labour relations arbitrators.

Jim holds four degrees, including a doctorate, has taught courses on organizational dynamics, innovation and facilitating strategic change at several Canadian and American universities, is a sought-after advisor on corporate renewal, a highly regarded specialist on governance and accountability, a mediator and former professor of International Law, a change agent with an enviable track record of accomplishments, and the list goes on.

Jim is CEO of **optimal solutions** *international*, a consulting practice dedicated to helping people and organizations reach their full potential. A father of four, he resides on his farm in central Ontario and spends his recreational time developing his gardens and tree plantations.

The **optimal***negotiator*©

Developed for the University of Alberta as its first Internet-based training program, The **optimal***negotiator*© enables students to create a customized learning experience on their own time that fits their needs and reflects their unique "negotiating quotient."

Features include a self-assessment tool, interactive simulation, responses to frequently asked questions, a library, opportunities to dialogue, and a dynamic resource centre with over 100 practical topics on negotiating.

The **optimal***negotiator*© may be taken for general interest study or credit against certificate programs offered by professional associations. Students may access the site as often as they wish within a specified time period. Former students are encouraged to return to re-evaluate and upgrade their skills.

For complete details, visit the site at *www.optimal-negotiator.com*.

optimal solutions *international*

Our mission is to help people and organizations reach their full potential by changing how they do business.

Our work focuses primarily on enhancing organizational dynamics and team effectiveness, on facilitating consensus and common cause among key stakeholders, and on finding innovative, strategic alternatives to existing business practices.

For a description of our capabilities and approach to solving organizational problems, designing business transformation strategies, and facilitating sustainable change, consult our corporate web site at *www.optimal-answers.com*.

For information on our executive development and management training programs, consult *www.optimal-learning.com*

To reach us:

E-mail: optimal@sentex.net
Phone: 519-924-2084
Fax: 519-924-2044

We make the optimal solution feasible.
We don't make the feasible solution optimal.

The Game of Life

"... uncanny insight on what makes people tick." – C.W.
"It's always in my briefcase ..." – C.H.G.
"One of the most rewarding books on maintaining important relationships I will likely ever read." – R.G.

Another great book by Dr. Jim Murray.

Discover how to befriend bullies, manage manipulators and tame tough guys. This timeless book outlines the guiding principles and rules for preventing turmoil in important relationships. It shows you how to get others to align with your personal and professional goals.

Learn how to win over bureaucrats, dinosaurs, know-it-alls, pessimists, wafflers, whiners, rebels and other challenging players – those who cause the greatest stress, conflict and wasted time in our lives. We know most of them. Which is why this reader friendly book's practical, every day examples are so helpful.

Understand the games people play and why normal emotional responses are ineffective. Find out how to benefit from human nature rather than fighting it. Learn how to get your work done without undue frustration, anger and confusion. Take back control of your life.

The Game of Life is available by pre-paid order. For a fax direct order form, contact the publisher, **optimal solutions** *international* (Fax: 519-924-2044; e-mail: *optimal@sentex.net*). Or check out *www.The-Game-of-Life.com*. VISA orders accepted.

Order Direct by mail, fax or e-mail

The **optimal**_negotiator_ and _The Game of Life_ are available by pre-paid order.

Ship to: _____
(Please print name)

_____
Complete Address

_____
(City)   (Prov./State)   (Zip/Postal Code)

Cost per book: (includes shipping, handling & applicable tax)
The **optimal**_negotiator: A Companion for Serious Deal Makers_
    Softcover: $34.95 (CDN) or $24.95 (US) _____

The Game of Life: Turning Conflict into Co-operation
    Softcover: $29.95 (CDN) or $22.95 (US) _____

    Hardcover: $39.95 (CDN) or $29.95 (US) _____

                            Amount Due $ _____

Payment: By cheque / money order or by VISA

_____
Card Number

_____
Expiry Date   Day Telephone Number

_____
Signature

To order by fax or mail, contact the publisher:
optimal solutions _international_, 347500 4th Concession, Maxwell ON, N0C 1J0. Fax: 519-924-2044. To order via e-mail, forward pertinent information to _optimal@sentex.net_.

Please enquire about discounts available on bulk orders.